Powell Lake by Barge and Quad
Coastal British Columbia Stories

Copyright © 2016 Wayne J. Lutz

All rights reserved. No part of this publication may be reproduced, stored in a retrieval system, or transmitted, in any form or by any means, electronic, mechanical, photocopying, recording, or otherwise, without the written prior permission of the author. Reviewers are authorized to quote short passages within a book review, as permitted under the United States Copyright Act of 1976.

Note for Librarians: a catalog record for this book that includes Dewey Decimal Classification and U.S. Library of Congress numbers is available from the Library and Archives of Canada. The complete catalog record can be obtained from their online database at:
www.collectionscanada.ca/amicus/index-e.html

ISBN 978-1-927438-20-6
Printed in the United States of America

Powell River Books
Powell RIver, BC
Book sales online at:
www.powellriverbooks.com
phone: 604-483-1704
email: wlutz@mtsac.edu

10 9 8 7 6 5 4 3 2 1

Powell Lake by Barge and Quad
Coastal British Columbia Stories

Wayne J. Lutz

2016
Powell River Books

To Western Forest Products...

The primary logging company on Powell Lake,

supporting barge ramps, docks, and logging

roads that open destinations of beauty.

The stories are true, and the characters are real.
Some details are adjusted to protect the guilty.
All of the mistakes rest solidly with the author.

Front Cover Photo:
  Near Dunn Dock, Powell Lake BC
Back Cover Photos
  Chip South, Powell Lake BC

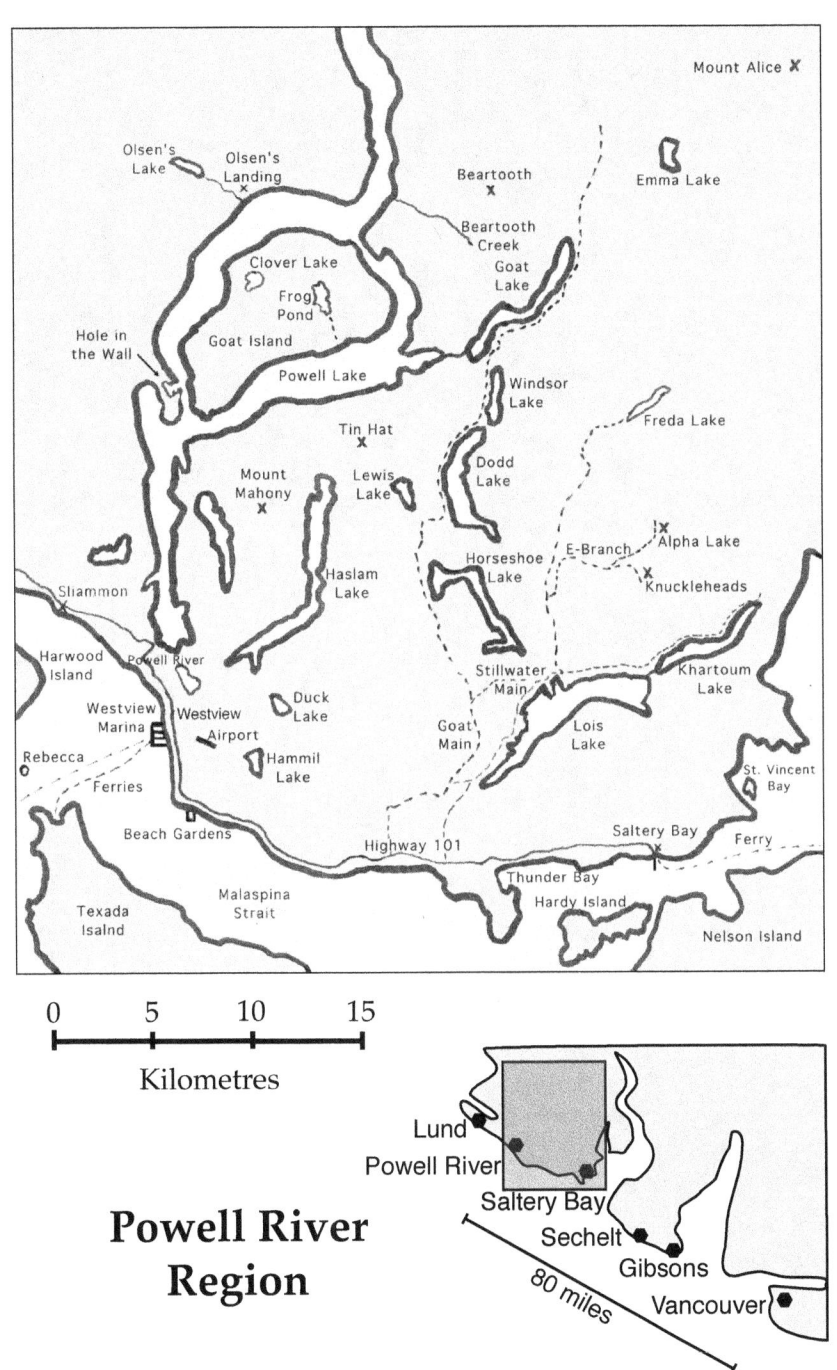

Powell River Region

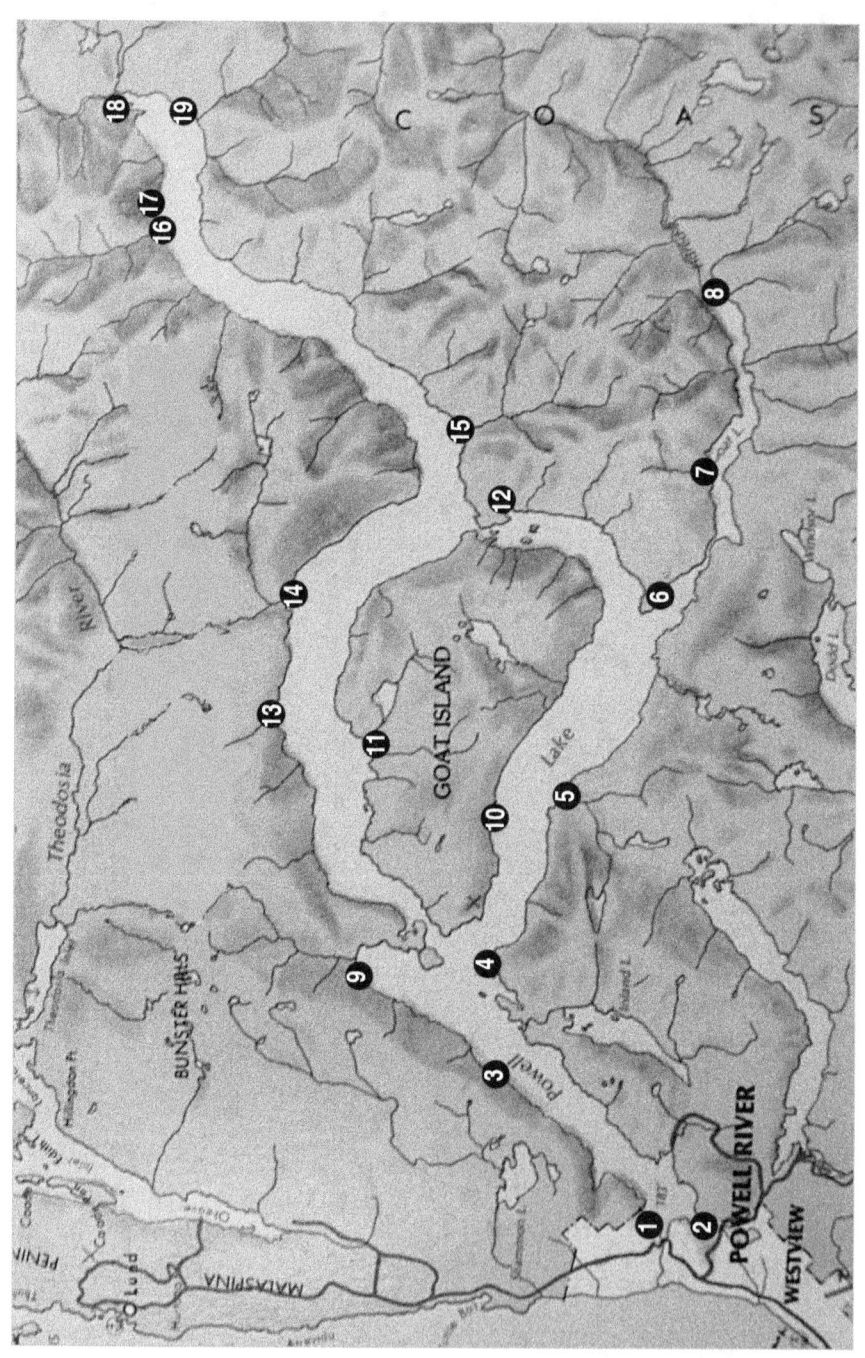

Powell Lake and Goat Lake Barge Ramps

1 – Shinglemill

2 – Mowat Bay

3 – Chipp South

4 – Pickle Point

5 – Fiddlehead Farm

6 – Narrows

7 – No Name (Narrows)

8 – No Name (Public Ramp)

9 – Chippewa Bay

10 – Dunn (Goat Island)

11 – Goat Island (Clover Main)

12 – Shermans (Rainbow Lodge)

13 – Chipp North

14 – Olsen's Landing

15 – Beartooth

16 – Billy Goat

17 – No Name (Billy Goat North)

18 – The Head (Daniels Main)

19 – Inactive (Jim Brown)

Legend – Barge Ramps

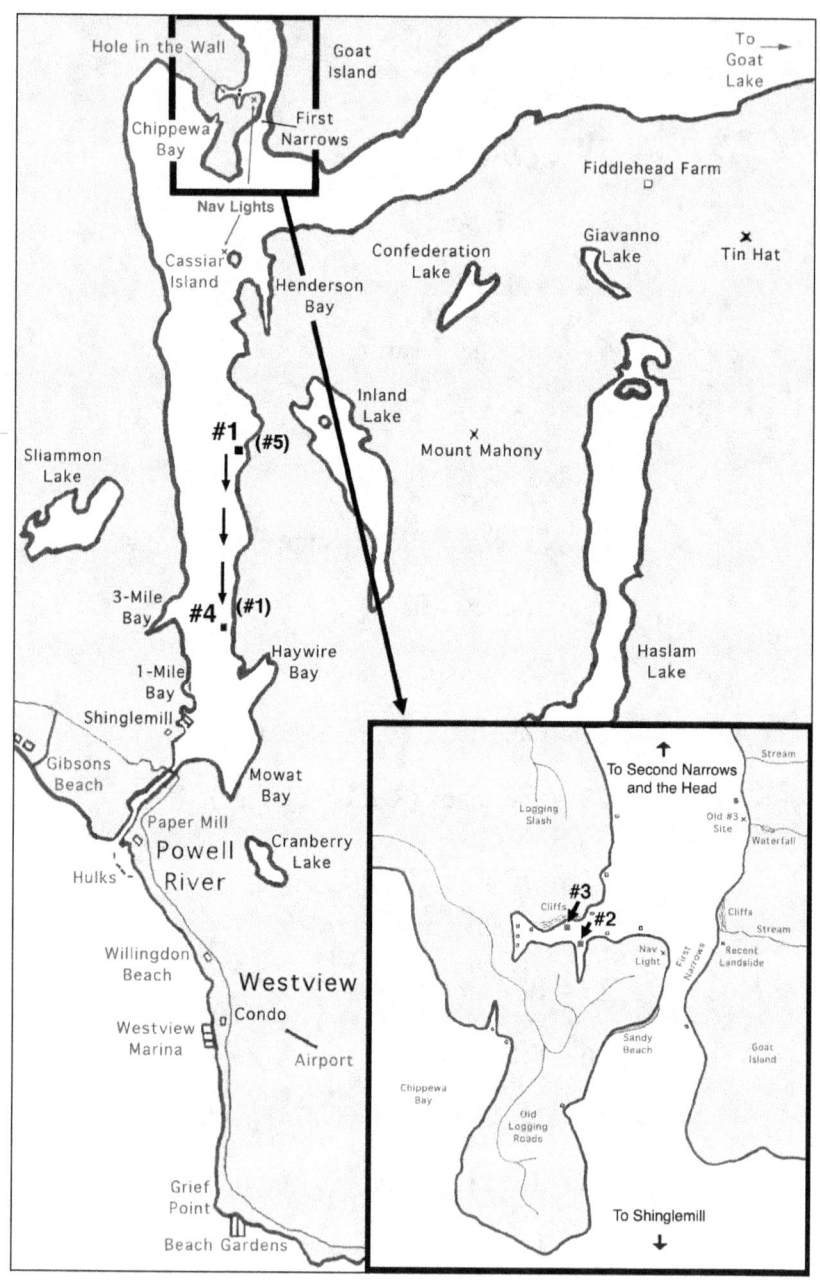

Lower Powell Lake

Books by Wayne J. Lutz

Coastal British Columbia Stories
Up the Lake
Up the Main
Up the Winter Trail
Up the Strait
Up the Airway
Farther Up the Lake
Farther Up the Main
Farther Up the Strait
Cabin Number 5
Off the Grid
Beyond the Main
Up the Inlet
Powell Lake by Barge and Quad
Islands and Inlets

Science Fiction Titles
Echo of a Distant Planet
Inbound to Earth
Across the Gallactic Sea
Anomaly at Fortune Lake
When Galaxies Collide

Pacific Northwest Series
Paddling the Pacific Northwest
Flying the Pacific Northwest

Contents

Preface – After *Beyond the Main* 12

1 – First Day of Summer. 14
    Goat Lake and Goat Main

2 – Sasquatch of Goat Lake 27
    Goat Lake and Goat Main

3 – Canada Day 36
    Shermans Main, Rainbow Lodge

4 – New Road in the Forest 50
    Chippewa South

5 – Looking for Spire Lake 57
    Dunn and Spire Main, Goat Island

6 – Old Haunts 71
    Fiddlehead Farm and a Myraid of Lakes

7 – Donkey Trail 86
    Above Museum Main, Chippewa Bay

8 – Chasing the Sun. 96
    Clover Dock, Goat Island

CENTER-OF-BOOK ILLUSTRATIONS 108

9 – 2-Trees	112
Spire Main, Goat Island	
10 – Cutting My Way Through	129
Chippewa North	
11 – An Early Touch of Summer	137
Olsen's Landing	
12 – Two Chips	147
Chippewa South and Chippewa North	
13 – Secret Spot	158
Theodosia Valley	
14 – Summer Traffic on Goat Main	166
Head of Goat Lake and No Name	
15 – Unexpected Destinations	176
Beartooth	
16 – The Head	185
Head of Powell Lake	
About the Author	205
Geographic Indexr	206

Preface

After *Beyond the Main*

BEYOND THE MAIN BEGAN WITH CHAPTERS about a long-time goal of mine – a trip to the head of Powell Lake with John, riding our quads over a three-day period into some of the most beautiful country imaginable. John and I (along with his trusty dog, Bro) made the journey by pushing a cedar log raft to carry our quads and camping gear, powered by my Campion bowrider – a slow but fabulous cruise.

Months later, Margy and I moved our quads to a remote parking area carved out of the forest near our floating cabin on Powell Lake. From there, we explored the region surrounding Chippewa Bay on day-rides. Theoretically, we could have traveled west into Theodosia Valley and then north to Olsen's Landing, but we never did. These more-distant destinations were just too far to be enjoyable without incorporating overnight camping. Pitching our tent in the open areas of bear and cougar country made us think twice.

So we looked for alternatives. Having our quads near our home on the lake was convenient, but not ideal. We considered purchasing a landing craft to carry our bikes to distant locations on Powell Lake, utilizing the barge ramps and docks maintained by Western Forest Products. Maybe we could even leave our quads permanently parked on a vessel like this. We also visualized pitching our tent in the landing craft during overnight trips, minimizing our concern regarding an unlikely (but it only takes once) attack by wild animals.

I looked for a landing craft for nearly two years. The few I found were overpriced, barely lake-worthy, or sold before I could phone the owner. Then I found a self-propelled "barge" that sounded perfect. Its design was different than a landing craft, with the entire deck platform raised. Metal ramps could be used to off-load our quads. And this design had an unexpected attribute. Without the upward slanting bow gate of a landing craft, there was increased deck space for our quads and tent.

As documented in *Beyond the Main*, Margy and I quickly adapted this barge to fulfill our dream of exploring Powell Lake's backcountry by quad – right from our cabin. During our first outings, we learned a lot about how to handle ramp off-loads and on-loads, and almost immediately we were camping on the deck. I promised myself that we'd soon return to the head of Powell Lake, but in the meantime, we looked forward to a lot of other territory to explore. And so the adventures began.

Quads on Barge at Hole in Wall

Chapter 1

First Day of Summer
Goat Lake and Goat Main

THE WEATHER HASN'T BEEN SUMMERLIKE. Margy and I planned to depart our floating cabin for Goat Lake this morning, but a torrential downpour interrupted loading the barge last night. Now the cold front has passed, and puffy cumulus clouds dot a bright blue sky. Mid-day temperatures are forecast to reach only 13 degrees, indicating a cold night ahead.

"What do you think?" I ask Margy, my wife and fellow barge adventurer on Powell Lake.

"I think we could wait until tomorrow, but I'm willing to go now. Gonna' be cold in the tent though."

It's amazing how similar we view things. It wasn't always this way, but since we've moved off the grid, our tendency to read each other's minds is uncanny.

"So let's stay home until tomorrow," I suggest. "Besides, it's another excuse to enjoy our cabin."

We love this place, our small floating home on Powell Lake, nestled against the steeply-cliffed entrance to Hole in the Wall. Any excuse for being here is considered valid, so we apply this logic all the time.

"If we get an early start tomorrow, we'll easily beat John to the barge ramp on Goat Lake," notes Margy. "We can eat breakfast along the way."

John is supposed to meet us on his quad at the head of Goat Lake at about noon tomorrow. I estimate a three-hour trip by barge, so it won't require a crack-of-dawn start for us. Officially, tomorrow is the first day of summer, with dawn coming mighty early. The extended sunlight is great for barging and quadding. But you'd think the longest days of the year would be a bit warmer.

* * * * *

THE NEXT MORNING, before departing Hole in the Wall, we need to move a big wooden spool with 180 feet of steel cable to the log raft that floats next to our breakwater log boom. At the moment, the spool sits on the bow of our barge, where it was loaded two days ago when we brought the cable up to our cabin for a repair project. That day, we arrived at our cabin in a rainstorm, so we've delayed the transfer to the raft until now. The heavy spool would be in our way during the trip to Goat Lake, so we'll drop it onto the raft before leaving.

The barge currently holds two quads, our overnight camping gear, four fishing poles, two loading ramps, three cans of fuel, an anchor, a spare 12-volt battery pack, lots of extra rope, spare clothing, and enough food and drinks for a week. Plus a big spool of cable.

This vessel is new to us, launched in Powell Lake for the first time only a month ago. We've already landed the barge at a variety of logging ramps, off-loaded our quads, and enjoyed several short but pleasurable rides. We've camped on the barge twice, and are getting used to maneuvering our bikes on and off under a variety of wind and wave conditions.

This morning, we've added our tin boat to the configuration. It's tied alongside for now. Once we're in open water, we'll allow it to trail out behind us on a 50-foot towing line. But first we'll need to get rid of the spool of cable. To do so, I need to turn the barge (with the attached tin boat) sharply within the confines of our breakwater boom, and maneuver it against the raft so we can push the spool of cable onto it safely (meaning – it won't float).

The front deck of the barge is slightly higher than the raft and overlaps it, so pushing the spool off is easier than expected. It's always nice when a challenging departure begins smoothly. With minimal time and effort, we're quickly outside the breakwater and on our way, with the tin boat now deployed behind us on its towline.

We motor south through First Narrows and turn left along the south side of giant Goat Island. It's a simple trip, with a quick stop to change configuration as we approach the entrance to Goat River. (Goat Island, Goat River, Goat Lake – goats everywhere around here.) I pull the tin boat forward and lash it tight against the bumper tires at the starboard side of the barge. In these favorable high water conditions, it will be fairly easy to maneuver up the meandering river that connects Powell Lake to Goat Lake. Dodging around snags, submerged stumps, and underwater shelves is routine today. Powell Lake typically fluctuates by 3 metres or more annually, mostly due to spring runoff and changes in the gates of the dam at the south end of the lake, and this month is one of our "high tides." But Goat River still deserves a slow speed and our full attention. I send Margy out onto the bow to watch for pockets of shallow water, while I monitor the depth sounder inside the cab. Every few minutes, she points her arm to the left or right to suggest a better heading.

We break out into Goat Lake. It's a lot smaller than Powell Lake, but the mountains are at least as majestic, particularly since they're confined to such a small space. Only three float cabins and two land cabins are located on this lake, and boat traffic is typically absent.

Our destination today is the head of the lake, near the outlet of the Eldred River. We'll be meeting John here at about noon, after he rides in from his quad off-load spot near Tin Hat Junction on lower Goat Main. The logging road continues north past the head of Goat Lake

Maneuvering through Goat River

into some of the most magnificent riding country in lower British Columbia.

John is our friend, off-the-grid mentor, and trail guide, but we haven't ridden with him in over a year. Now, with a barge to access some of the more established trails in the area, we'll be able to ride with him more often. He recently bought a new King Quad, after finally trading in his trusty ol' Grizz. Bro's rear box has been moved over to the new quad, but the Labrador retriever is now 14 years old, and showing his age. He still rides everywhere with John, but it's obviously a struggle for the huge dog. We've watched Bro grow up from an energetic pup, and it's sad to see him age and drag his heavy body around on his increasingly weak hind legs, typical of aging Labs.

After steering clear of Goat River, we leave the tin boat tied to the side of the barge, where it seems to tow fine at cruise speed in these nearly calm conditions. We'll learn this is the simplest way to tote the small boat, except in rough wave conditions when it rides better on its 50-foot aft tether.

We cruise past the barge ramp called "No Name," a place we plan to visit someday soon. The nearby Narrows ramp on Powell Lake is normally connected to No Name via Narrows Main, but the old logging road is now washed out. So we'll need No Name to gain access to the eastern regions on this side of Goat Lake. As we pass No Name, Margy and I discuss how we'll off-load our quads here when the time comes. There's no dock at No Name, but we can see a spot along the shore where we can tie up to a snag. Since this area is seldom used by anyone, we would probably feel comfortable leaving the barge at the ramp while we're riding, and not inconveniencing anybody.

Passing the halfway point on Goat Lake, we look up at the bluff. We can see the viewpoint where quads stop to look down on the lake. There's no sign of John waiting for us here, but we hear a motor approaching at a high speed behind us. I gaze back to see a boat that looks like a landing craft about to pass our barge.

"Oh, oh," I say to Margy. "It looks like Trapper Jim, and I bet he's headed to the barge ramp at the head of the lake."

I know Jim visits this area often, sometimes with a quad aboard. The temporary dock at the head of the lake, built by our friend Bob, is probably gone by now. Where will two large boats tie up?

"I don't think he has any quads on board," notes Margy.

She's right. As Trapper Jim passes, it's obvious his landing craft contains no quads.

"He sees us with our quads, and its obvious where we're headed," I say. "So I'm sure he won't leave his boat at the ramp."

"It'll work out," says Margy. And it always does.

Trapper Jim disappears out of sight around the bend in the lake, propelled by his big outboard motor. In comparison, our barge is a slow poke, but we've come to enjoy traveling at only 7 knots. I know I could never adjust to a slow trawler on the ocean. As the saying goes: "Once you've been on plane, you'll find it hard to slow down." But I've discovered unique contentment in this barge. Undoubtedly, it's because I'm motoring slowly in a region I love so much.

As we pass the next promontory, there's Trapper Jim's landing craft, beached on the north shore of the lake, far from the barge ramp. Maybe he's out for a hike today.

"Looks like a woman with him," says Margy. "And Jim's carrying a gun."

So that's it. Probably Jim was never planning to go to the barge ramp at all. He's hunting or checking his trap lines along the shore and up into the hills.

As we approach our destination at the head of Goat Lake, we first slow to examine the shore near the outlet of the Eldred River. We find an old log dump here, but no barge ramp or dock. Still, we decide it'll be worth our while to tie up here someday. Then we can hike along the old overgrown road that leads along the shore, and eventually past the tree-choked dirt runway that's been closed for more than a decade.

As we angle towards the empty barge ramp, it's obvious the old dock is gone. Fortunately a huge snag lies just offshore, where the dock was originally tied up.

"I'm going out to get things ready for off-load," I say to Margy. "Just keep us headed towards the ramp. Go slow, so I have enough time."

The barge ramp still seems a long way ahead, but I've got a lot to do. Over the past few weeks, Margy and I have learned how to quickly get our quads off and back on the barge. Still, we learn something new each time. One thing that's been obvious from the beginning – it's important to get everything ready well before we hit the shore, particularly if we expect wind or waves. Even though there's hardly a breeze today, I start through my preparation.

First, I unstrap the quads and remove the chocks. Then I pull the metal ramps forward so they sit on the bow with about a third protruding outward. These skookum ramps are heavy, so it's best to get part of their weight extended out front, ready to pull to shore.

I make sure the ignition keys are in the quads, and the fuel shut-off levers are positioned "on." Now I start up both quads, to give the engines plenty of time to warm up. I look up and see the shore approaching sooner than expected, and I notice Margy has shifted into neutral to give me more time to get things finished. But now I'm ready, or am I?

"Don't forget your water shoes," yells Margy, as she leans out the cab door.

"Oh, right."

Best laid plans. Gloves and water shoes are "nice-to-haves" for the off-load process. At least I remembered my gloves.

I step back into the cab to change shoes, while we float motionless about 10 metres from shore.

"Anything special you want me to do?" asks Margy, as she relinquishes the helm, and I shift into forward gear.

"No, but you can go out onto the deck now, and be ready with the pike pole, in case it's needed" I reply. "Pretty calm today, but if things go astray, be ready to hop back into the cab. When I go out onto the deck to drop the ramps to shore, I'll leave the engine running, with the motor raised pretty high. If you need to back out, be sure to drop the outboard down to get full reverse thrust once you're in deeper water."

"Okay, she says. "Do you need help with the ramps?"

"I'll be okay. I'd rather have you standing by with the pike pole in case we start to drift."

We work well together. This barge has been a good chance to practice teamwork.

As we glide straight towards the beach, I proceed slowly in forward gear, and then shift into neutral. Margy exits the cab, to take her position on the deck with the pike pole. I raise the leg high enough to keep the prop in a safe position, but not so high that cooling water stops circulating through the outboard. I know we're okay, as long as water spurts from the leg's outlet hole. The depth sounder reads 6 feet, and the shallow water alarm begins to beep.

I step out onto the deck now, where Margy is already holding the pike pole, ready to push off the shallow bottom to keep us straight. A faint *crunch* marks the moment the bow touches shore, and the barge comes to a halt. I hop off onto dry ground, no need for my water shoes yet, but it's good to be ready. I quickly pull the metal ramps into position, lining them up for the wheels of the quads. Once the first ramp is firmly down, the barge won't drift unless there's a crosswind. With the second ramp down, we can relax and take things slowly. Margy doesn't even need to dip her pole into the water.

I drive the first quad off the barge, backing down the ramp. When I try to continue backing up the rock-strewn incline, the wheels spin. There's just enough traction on this steep slope to back far enough to make room for the second quad. I know these transmissions are low torque in reverse without four-wheel drive engaged, so I just spin my wheels, slowly working my way uphill. As usual, I'm comfortable taking the lazy way out, throwing a little dirt in the process.

Goat Lake Off-Load

I stop and take a moment to enjoy the scenery. Looking back at the barge, I see Margy standing by the second quad, looking content, with beautiful Goat Lake in the background. In these calm conditions, with both metal ramps in the dirt, there's no hurry to do anything.

With the second quad off-loaded, Margy helps me pull the first ramp aboard. I suspect the boat might begin to drift sideways when I remove the second ramp.

"Go back to the cab now," I suggest. "As soon as I have the other ramp aboard, you can begin to back away from shore. It's plenty deep here, so lower the leg down all the way for maximum power in reverse."

All goes flawlessly. Margy backs away from shore as I give the bow a small, unneeded push, and hop aboard. We stop just offshore, discussing where to park for the night. At first we plan to pull parallel to the shore, and secure the boat there. Then we decide to come straight in, offset slightly from the barge ramp, tying the bow to shore. Then we can back away far enough to tie a line to the big snag behind us. It's similar to a stern-tie anchorage, except our rear end is facing outward, and there's no anchor involved.

I maneuver the barge straight towards shore, but a little too fast, and the bow crunches more than desired. Although this tough metal boat can take some real abuse, this is more than anything I've experienced so far. I notice that some bottom paint has rubbed off onto the rocks.

"Oh, oh," I say to Margy. "John's gonna' see that blue paint on shore."

"He'll never notice," she teases, knowing John never misses anything.

I tie the bow to a heavy steel cable that's already wound around a big rock (probably from the old logging days), and push off with my arms to drift towards the snag 10 metres behind us. As we float slowly back towards the snag, I struggle to fasten some ropes together for the stern-tie. I have enough ropes, but it requires several connections.

"I hear quads," says Margy.

"Can't be John," I reply. "It's only 10:30. He said he wouldn't be here until noon."

"I bet it's him," she quips.

And she's right. While I'm still struggling with the ropes, John appears around the corner from Goat Main, accompanied by another quad and a blue Jeep bringing up the rear.

John stops close to shore, while the Jeep and other quad park on the opposite side of the main.

"Hey, John! We didn't expect you so early," I yell. "We just got here."

"Just now?" he says. "I thought you camped here last night."

"No, it was rainy and cold, so we waited until this morning."

When you ride with John, it's best not to dawdle. He'll rush you along, even if everything is ahead of schedule. Today, I'm already beginning to feel behind schedule, although technically I'm early.

"Can I give you a hand?" he says.

"Sure," I say. "I've just finished tying the stern to a snag behind us."

As usual, John jumps right in, and everything gets squared away almost immediately. He adjusts the bowline so the barge is more secure. Then he reaches out seemingly farther than human arms should extend, and pulls one of the metal ramps to shore, resting it on a hefty rock. In just a few minutes, we're able to walk right off the barge on a makeshift narrow bridge he's instantly constructed.

"I'd planned to use the tin boat to get to shore," I explain. "This will be even better."

I notice John looking down into the water, where surely he must see the fresh blue paint on the rocks. He doesn't say anything, but there's no doubt what he's thinking.

"It'll take us just a few minutes to get ready to ride," I say.

"No problem," he replies. "Take your time."

I know he doesn't mean it.

"See, John didn't notice the blue paint," I say quietly to Margy.

"Oh, he saw it," she replies. "He just didn't mention it."

By now, John's brother, Dave, has appeared from the Jeep, accompanied by his wife, Jayne. They stand talking at the barge ramp near our parked boat, while Margy and I don our riding gear. John points towards the ground near the ramp, noting something in the dirt. Meanwhile, Brent, the fellow on the other quad, is already fishing from shore.

"Look, Dave," says John, still examining the dirt near the ramp. "The scruff of those tire tracks are what happens when you try to back uphill in a quad without using four-wheel drive. Not much torque in reverse without it."

"Uh-huh," replies Dave.

I know these words are meant for me, not Dave, but I don't say anything. You can never hide from John.

This isn't how I'd planned it. Ideally, I expected to be off-loaded well in advance of John's arrival, so I'd have plenty of time to get ready to ride. Instead, we've barely arrived, and it's time to get going. Still, riding with John is <u>always</u> a fantastic experience. There's nothing else like it, as I've learned time and time again over the past decade. Today is no exception.

As we ride behind John and the Jeep, Margy and I are feeling a little rushed as the vehicles in front of us roll out of sight. Meanwhile I look back, and Brent is on the quad behind us, pushing up seemingly close. Margy and I can't seem to keep up the pace, and it starts to get to me. So I stop to let Brent catch up.

"Go ahead, if you want to," I tell Brent.

"I'm okay in back," he replies. "Take your time."

At least now, I feel we're not holding up the entire group, but John isn't about to slow down until we get to our destination, Squirrel Creek. Goat Main's bridge over this big stream was deactivated several years ago, after logging to the north was (for now) completed. It's a matter of logging company liability policy to prevent public injuries on their unused roads. It wouldn't be surprising to see this bridge reconstructed to provide access to future timber cuts. Until then, there are still lots of places to ride near the creek, and this is one of John's favourite areas for exploration on his quad.

Along the way to Squirrel Creek, we pass magnificent waterfalls plunging down from the mountains on our right, running under bridges to drop nearly vertically into the mighty Eldred River. I know Margy would love to stop and take some pictures, but she doesn't want to fall farther behind John. But she finally pulls to a halt in front of me, and I pull up next to her.

"Better not be taking time for pictures!" I scold her kiddingly.

"Getting cold. Got to zip up my jacket," she says.

"I'm gonna' tell John you stopped," I tease. "I'll tell him you took extra time to stop and zip up your jacket."

She puts out her tongue, and gives me an ugly (but humourous) frown.

By now, Brent has pulled up next to us. He's the teenage son of a friend of John's. This kid really knows the outdoors, and understands John quite well.

"She stopped to zip her jacket," I say to Brent. "Don't tell John."

Brent looks at me with a confused look. Maybe he doesn't know John as well as I thought. Or maybe it's that pesky generation gap.

Our next stop occurs because we've left Goat Main on a minor unmarked spur, and Dave and Jayne can go no farther in their Jeep. The trail has narrowed considerably and now turns into a rugged path only passable by quad or on foot. John is disappearing down the rough trail on his quad, and Brent pulls around to follow him. Margy is shaking her head, and I know what that means.

"How far do you think John is going?" I ask Dave.

"Not far. We've been here before, and it's an easy hike to the end of the trail, about a 15-minute walk. Follow us."

"Good, then we'll walk, too."

Margy and I follow Dave and Jayne along the rutted path, barely good enough for a quad. The terrain is pretty rugged, even on foot.

When we finally catch up with John and Brent, they're parked at Squirrel Creek. John sits on his quad eating a sandwich, while Brent fishes from a small cliff above the roaring rapids. This is a spot John visits a lot, and I can see why. He tends to conceal his favourite destinations from others in an attempt to keep them secluded, but he's always quick to share them with friends. If you want the exact location, you'll need to ask John, and I bet he'll tell you. I won't!

For John, just finding this private spot was a goal not for the feint of heart. As usual this time, he persisted, exploring until he found the perfect location. His love of the outdoors and relentless pursuit of extreme beauty show his intense dedication to the mountains of this region. That's one of the many things that make me intensely proud to call John my friend.

After spending some time relaxing here, absorbing the sublime remoteness, we follow the trail back to our quads in the clearing. From there, Margy and I head back to our barge. John and the others are heading up Dianne Main. Several years ago, Margy tried riding up

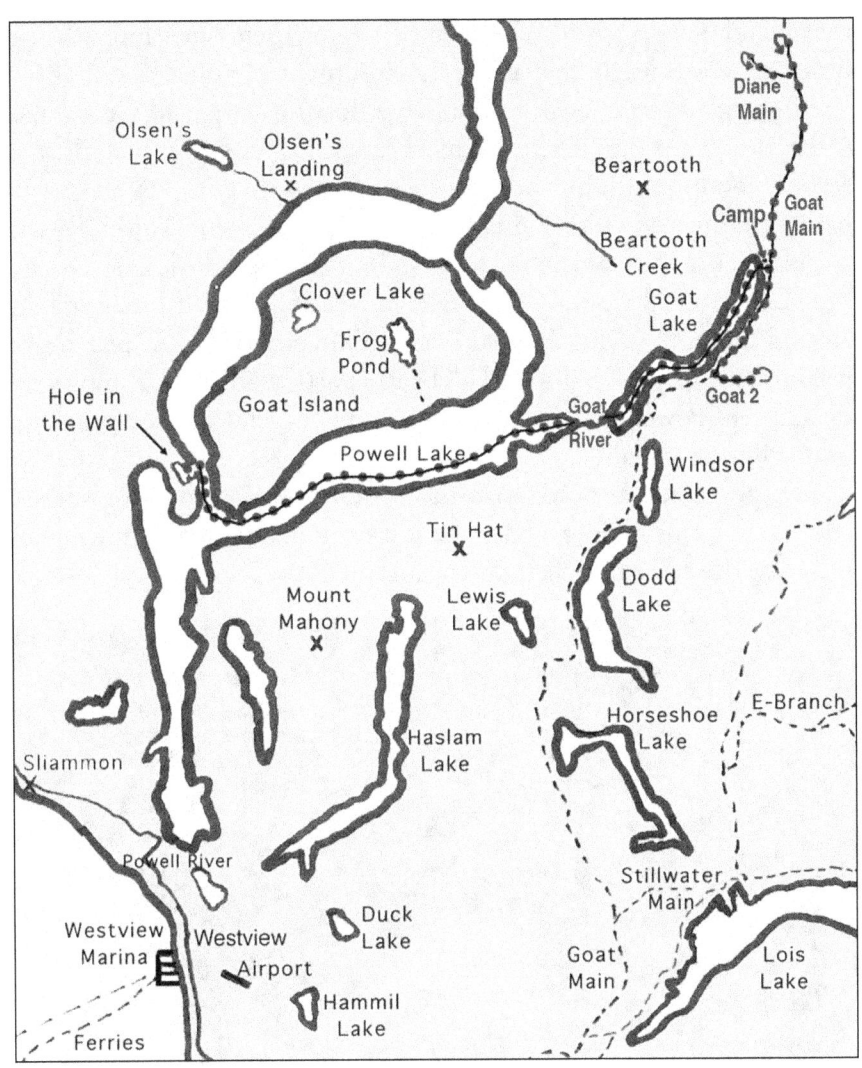

Goat Lake Trip

there, and its steep terrain doesn't bring back pleasant memories for her. John seems to understand, so we say our temporary farewells.

The trip back down the main is more relaxed. We stop at several places to take pictures, and ride slowly and to take in the beauty of the mountains, including the sheer cliffs on the far side of the Eldred where rock climbers flock for a taste of an extended vertical wall ascent. We stop to try to look for climbers on the granite cliffs, but we don't see any. They could be there, but unless you know exactly where to look, they blend in with the cliff. I remember seeing them once, looking like little ants crawling on the face of the mountain.

We're glad to get back to the barge floating on placid Goat Lake. After setting up our tent, we enjoy a relaxing evening, including a second goodbye to John and the other riders as they stop by the barge before heading down to Tin Hat Junction and home to Powell River.

Near sunset, we fish on the longest day of the year, June 21st. Margy catches one small trout, while I catch a tree and wrap my fishing line around the prop of our tin boat (while it's in gear). You'd expect more fish in a lake like this, although it's been a particularly poor fishing year on adjacent Powell Lake. Such things come in cycles, and are generally impossible to explain.

We go to bed at peace with the world. There's something special about being this far away from the rest of humanity, and knowing all is well at the end of the first day of summer.

Camping at Goat Lake

◊ ◊ ◊ ◊ ◊ ◊ ◊

Chapter 2

Sasquatch of Goat Lake
Goat Lake and Goat Main

THE NIGHT THAT SEPARATES the first and second days of summer at the head of Goat Lake is noteworthy because of a unique noise that awakens me. It sounds like something plopping into the water near the barge. Once I'm awake, I lie listening for more, and soon hear what sounds like a large rock plunging into the water from a great height. This time it comes from behind the barge. This is a bit disconcerting because I can think of only one logical source – a human throwing rocks into the lake in the middle of the night. But there's no sound of rustling near the beach, and I've heard no motor vehicle approach.

Another rock! It hits with a loud *thunk* rather than the softer *kerplunk* common when fish jump out of the water and flop back in.

Margy seems to be sound asleep, and I don't need to awaken her to verify I'm really hearing these sounds. There's no doubt in my mind that this is real. One more *thunk*, and everything is still. After some puzzling thoughts I go back to sleep. I'm convinced no humans are nearby, and any critter making these repeated sounds would be extremely unusual, whether fish or land animal. The most fearful creature is man, and it doesn't seem to be a human that's involved.

John would be a prime suspect, if I didn't know he was at home, for it's his kind of joke, and nothing else makes sense. I'm not one to become alarmed while sleeping outdoors in remote locations, but when I wake up in the morning, I'm surprised that Margy brings up the unusual noise first. She was awake when I thought she was asleep, and has an immediate answer to the weird sounds: "It's obviously Sasquatch," she says matter-of-factly.

We kid about how Sasquatch probably has a great sense of humour, and loves to scare camping humans. This is certainly the perfect place to do it. Both Margy and I heard trees rustling the previous evening in different locations – she above our barge and I along the shore while fishing. Neither of us mentioned the noise in the trees because we both assumed it was the natural action of wildlife in such a pristine location, but we mention it now.

We come to no solid conclusions, so Sasquatch is a light-hearted explanation that satisfies both of us. We're just glad that we've concluded it's not one of those scary humans.

"I bet we remember where we were on the second day of summer," notes Margy.

"At the head of Goat Lake," I reply.

"And listening for Sasquatch," she chides.

While still in the tent talking, I hear a truck pull to a stop on Goat Main, right above us.

"Must be a logger looking for coffee," I say to Margy.

A few minutes later, while looking out the window of the tent, I see a logger dressed in an orange reflective vest, with a radio and ear protectors dangling from his belt. I climb out of the tent to greet him.

He introduces himself as the helicopter logging ground supervisor from Dianne Main, headed to work. He's interested in our evaluation of the fishing conditions in the lake. We're more interested in the whole concept of heli-logging.

"Been in this business for thirty years," he says. "Costs ten thousand dollars per hour for big logging helicopters these days, but trees are worth more now, too – five thousand for a big cedar. My men top the tall trees in preparation for the helicopter, and then cut around the girth of the trunk almost all the way through. The helicopter lowers a big grappler, and tugs the tree side-to-side until it snaps off. Then we haul them down the mountain to the log sort. You'll see our trucks going by later today, headed for Stillwater.

"I live in Campbell River," he continues, "but spend most nights in Powell River while I'm on duty. I fly to work in one of the smaller choppers almost every day, except today I decided to drive. So tell me about the fishing here."

"Not very good," I reply. "Margy caught a small one last night, but I caught a tree."

"Caught three?" he says.

"No, I caught a tree. And a prop, too."

He laughs. I really enjoy talking to him, a nature lover who gets to experience the great outdoors every day in his job as a logging supervisor. He seems fascinated by Margy and me, impressed by our off-the-grid lifestyle in a floating cabin on Powell Lake. It's a friendship cemented immediately, with none of us even exchanging names. I'm sorry to see him leave.

After breakfast and a leisurely morning, we ride our quads up Goat Main to the intersection with Dianne Main. We cross the big bridge over the Eldred River, and start uphill. After Margy's previous bad experience with the climb beyond here, we don't expect to go very far. Soon we encounter a huge metal gate, now swung fully open. I remember being here ten years ago with Poki, one of the Powell River ATV Club's most famous members. When we encountered the locked gate, he pulled out a key loaned to him by one of his many logging buddies, and opened it so we could ride up Dianne Main. Soon after passing this gate, Margy wanted to turn back because of the precipitous road.

We ride a little farther, and encounter a pullout where we can look across the road to a landing pad with a bright yellow chopper from Powell River's Oceanview Helicopters. This is one of the crew transport choppers that brings logging crews into and out of the area each day.

With our engines turned off, we watch the activity at the landing pad. I can hear the buzz of chainsaws and then the crack of trees as they crash to the ground far up the valley. We wait a few minutes, and watch the helicopter as it takes off and heads up the deep valley between towering peaks. This route leads to the remote site where the crews are ready to start home at 2:30 on this Sunday afternoon. Loggers' days start and end early in the prolonged summer daylight, with weekend logging on Dianne Main an indicator of how well the lumber industry is thriving right now. Business is booming.

The loggers leave town for work at daybreak on long summer days like this, and finish mid-afternoon for the helicopter ride back down to the staging area on Goat Main. From there, it's a long truck ride home to Powell River.

Helicopter at Diane Main

With the helicopter now gone, Margy and I head back down Goat Main, stopping at the popular spot on the Eldred River where the water runs over sheer granite outcrops, carving its way through the rock. This is where John, as a teenager, was swept downstream, and somehow survived to tell about it. (By now, you've probably noticed that John is the protagonist in this series of books. It's hard to ignore a character so strong and representative of the spirit and spunk of coastal British Columbia.)

I spend some time lying on the granite slabs adjacent to the rushing Eldred, dozing but not really sleeping. Margy uses the time to photograph some of the wildflowers and berries surrounding the nearby public trail.

We return to the road and continue down Goat Main again, passing the sign that reminds us not to relax around here: "Rock Slide – Do not stop next 50 metres." The big boulders accumulated on the uphill side of the road attest to the power of rocks when they fall.

Following Margy down the main, I use our agreed-upon signal to get her to stop. We normally run with our headlights on, and when I turn mine off, Margy will notice the change in her rearview

Eldred River Viewpoint

mirror and come to a halt. Just to be sure that she notices my lights-off condition, I slow down briefly and let her ride out of sight. If she doesn't see me in her mirror for an extended period of time, she'll definitely stop. It works. When I start forward again, Margy has come to a standstill right around the bend, waiting for me to reappear. She holds her position while I pull up beside her.

"It's only a short distance back to the barge, and it's still early," I say over the sound of our engines. "How about trying Goat 2 today?"

"Okay," she says, but she sounds reluctant.

We've discussed going up Goat 1 or Goat 2 on this trip, but this morning we agreed to put it off until tomorrow. I can't remember which of these two secondary logging roads is in the best condition. One is supposedly in excellent shape for riding, and the other is an overgrown, trenched-cut disaster. I know Margy is avoiding them both, since she remembers these trails as precipitous. Once she gets into a "too steep" mindset, it's difficult for her to feel comfortable until conditions prove conclusively otherwise. Still, we've got lots of time left to give one of these trails a try.

"I think Goat 2 is first, with its turnoff just before the quad viewpoint."

"Okay," she replies, but she still sounds hesitant.

"Why don't you continue to lead past Goat 2, and we'll stop at the viewpoint," I say. "Then we can discuss what to do."

"Sure," she replies, sounding more confident about this plan.

So we continue down Goat Main, keeping an eye out for the turnoff that marks either Goat 1 or Goat 2. We pass a logging spur that might be one of these trails, except there are branches strewn across the entry. It might only go up to a slash, and the limbs are there simply because its been unused lately or someone has left a message that it's best not to enter.

Margy slows almost to a stop at this junction, and then accelerates ahead down the main. Within less than a kilometre, we pass another intersection, and this definitely looks like one of the Goat auxiliary roads that I rode a long time ago. Margy stops here, and I pull up alongside.

"I think this is Goat 2," I suggest.

"Deep ditch," she says, nodding towards the cross-trench that's obvious right at the beginning of the climb.

Big trenches like this serve one of two purposes (sometimes both) – an attempt to divert flowing water that's not severe enough to require a bridge, or it's the logging company's signature of a closed road. Once tree cutting is complete, the road may be deactivated to keep recreational vehicles out. Later, when the loggers re-enter for new ventures, it's easy for their road builders to fill in the trenches.

"Let's go to the viewpoint, and discuss it," I reply.

At the overlook, we shut off our engines, and enjoy a snack of granola bars and juice. Margy is reluctant to try the climb up the road with the prominent trench, but agrees to give it a try. So we retrace our path back to the junction – we're still not sure whether it's Goat 1 or 2 – and start uphill.

In cases like this, I prefer to let Margy lead, since she knows her limits, and is quick to admit them. After the first ditch, which she successfully negotiates, she stops before the next cross-trench. I know she's already in four-wheel drive, and this cut isn't beyond her abilities.

But she seems convinced this isn't going to work out, and it doesn't. When she drives down into the next deep cut, she stops before starting up on the other side. After a brief pause while she thinks about the situation, she accelerates upward, overcorrects a bit too much in her steering, and veers to the right side of road at the top of the trench. She doesn't go off the road, but it's close, and it's obvious that our trip has ended.

"No problem turning around," I say, after getting off my quad and hiking out of the trench myself, joining her at the top of the rise.

"I'd like to turn around," she replies. "But I'd rather not take my bike back down."

"Sure. I'll drive it down," I say.

Margy walks back down through the two ditches, which isn't easy on foot, especially climbing up on the far side. I wait for her to clear each trench before driving her quad down behind her. In a few minutes, we're back at the junction. I walk back up to retrieve my quad while Margy waits for me.

"I'm pretty sure this is Goat 2, so Goat 1 is the better road," I say when we're back together again on the edge of Goat Main.

"But not today," she says.

"Not today," I agree. "Let's go back to the barge, and enjoy the rest of the afternoon."

She smiles, obviously relieved that our climbing escapades are over for today. There will be plenty of opportunities to explore the roads branching off Goat Main some other day.

* * * * *

SASQUATCH DOESN'T COME TO VISIT AGAIN, and the next morning we laugh about how convinced we were regarding someone (something) throwing rocks into the water. It seems obvious the noise must have been from big fish jumping out of the water – which is surprising because we haven't found any sizable fish interested in our lures. But in the back of our minds.....

Early in the morning, shortly after 6 am, big trucks charge up Goat Main on their way to the log dumps along Dianne Main. This means they should start coming back southbound with heavy loads later in the morning.

Sure enough, I hear the first log hauler barreling down Goat Main just before 9 am. In an area this quiet, the sound of shifting gears and grinding tires can be heard well in advance. This first truck slows as it approaches our barge, and then I hear its air brakes announcing a complete stop. I pull on my shoes and rush to shore from the barge.

Before I arrive at the road, the truck has come to a halt. A driver in an orange vest is at the rear of the huge vehicle, inspecting his load. I walk to the back to greet him, wondering if he will be surprised at a visitor here in the middle of nowhere.

"Mighty big logs," I say. "Aren't you afraid the top row won't stay on?"

The highest row of logs is piled well above the metal guards on the sides of the truck. To me, these logs look like they could tumble off at any moment.

"No big deal," he says. "Sometimes I carry bigger loads." He answers as if someone is always walking up to him at a turnout on Goat Main to strike up a conversation.

"Bigger than as big as they can get?" I kid.

Logging Truck from Diane Main

He laughs, and crawls back into the cab of his truck by hoisting himself onto the huge running board and then farther up to the seat. He smiles at me, and I give him a thumbs-up.

"Now you be careful," I say as he shifts into gear.

The driver laughs, and gives a trumpeting blast of his air brakes. His big truck rumbles down Goat Main, while I listen to it disappear into the distance.

There's something very special about wilderness logging roads. They lead to wonderful adventures for both loggers and recreational travelers like me. And everyone you meet carries a smile because there's whole lot to smile about.

Chapter 3

Canada Day
Shermans Main, Rainbow Lodge

When it comes to summer holidays, Coastal BC seems jinxed. How often have Margy and I lamented for the dejected campers at Haywire Bay who were looking forward to their first family outing of the upcoming summer season on Victoria Day (near the end of May), only to find a traditional rainy weekend? This year's Victoria Day is no different, and Canada Day weekend in early July has followed suit. As John's dad, Ed, explained to me once: "There are two seasons in Canada – Winter and July 1st." Even that isn't true this year, so far.

As far as weather is concerned, Canada Day weekend is a bust. Since the July 1st holiday is on Tuesday this year, we expect considerable recreational traffic on Powell Lake the weekend before, but it doesn't develop. Rare severe thunderstorms Friday night and Saturday morning keep boaters at home in Powell River.

Over the weekend, a few lookie-loo's brave the elements, making their first summer excursion into Hole in the Wall. It's a common route for many travelers on the lake, either on their way to or from their cabins, since the Hole is on the list of natural (and human) attractions. The primary interest of these visitors is the hidden back-bay, where a lookie-loo will be treated to whatever changes have occurred since last season. This year, there are quite a few changes to greet them, with Bob (who we refer to by his boat's name, *Private Dancer*) beginning to build a replacement cabin on a nice, new float. Meanwhile, Cameron (known to us by the name of his boat, *Miss Budwiser*, and his family simply as the Texadans) has piles of wood stored on his deck, awaiting a major summer renovation project. Last weekend, the Texadans – from Texada Island – turned Margy and me into lookie-loo's, when the lumber arrived one evening on a new (to us) pontoon barge named *Huckleberry Fairy*.

This year, our floating cabin at the entrance to Hole in the Wall will be under special inspection, as lookie-loo's encounter our new barge with two quads on top. On this lake, a new vessel or cabin enhancement never goes unnoticed. Like everyone else, we pay close attention to every new boat and all visible changes to cabins. Lookie-loo's – all of us!

The forecast for Canada Day (Tuesday) is encouraging. After the winter-like storm over the weekend, Monday morning arrives sunny and bright. I phone Western Forest Products to inquire about the week's logging activity on the lake, but there's no answer, and I'm routed to voicemail. No surprise – this is probably a 4-day holiday for some of the logging supervisors, and those who are working are… well, working. As is often the case, the supervisors are out and about early each day at logging sites. They won't receive their messages until later in the day, and by then Margy and I will be gone.

When I checked last week, today's preferred destination, Shermans Main near Rainbow Lodge, was inactive. Things change fast in the logging business, and activity at this location seems to have quickly cooled off in recent weeks.

I know almost nothing about this barge ramp location, which makes it particularly enticing. From the Narrows log dump far to the south, where we recently camped on our barge, I noticed extensive logging roads winding southward from the Rainbow Lodge area. And the map shows additional roads leading north towards Beartooth. The only credible data I've obtained about this area is from Rod, a local photographer and hiker who tried to explore Shermans Main on foot recently. He reports the hike was "severely uphill," so he finally gave up. But a steep hiking hill may be easily conquered on a quad, unless it's so steep that it conquers Margy first. Certainly, it's worth a closer look.

The lodge itself is a historic landmark on the lake, originally an elaborate recreational facility for Powell River's paper mill. Stories abound regarding the "old days" when visiting mill executives were wined and dined at this elaborate facility near Second Narrows. After this celebrated period in the paper mill's bygone era, the lodge went up for sale over a decade ago. Part of the property was logged for private profit, an action criticized by some local citizens. Rainbow was a victim of comparison to what happened during the previous clear-cut stripping of communal Fiddlehead Farm when it was sold. However, the area logged at Rainbow Lodge was considerably smaller, and not nearly the eyesore, so the incident was soon forgotten.

After a period of inactivity, Rainbow Lodge became a retreat for students of the outdoor educational program of the local school district. The boat travel distance to the lodge from town was partly to blame for the lack of success during this interlude, a common factor that's thwarted many enterprising ideas on this lake. In recent years, Rainbow Lodge has faded from the local news, but it remains a major geographic icon for everyone on the Powell Lake. Elvis Point, Hole in the Wall, and Beartooth hold similar significance as locator symbols in the minds of those who travel on the lake.

This morning, before we depart, one cabin project remains – wildlife relocation at Cabin Number 3 (the designation for our home – the third of five cabins John has built on Powell Lake). Margy's floating garden has been under continuous attack for the past month, with something mowing down the veggies, including peas and beans in deck pots. It's a major invasion, unlike any previous year, and we're struggling to identify the culprits. So far, we've live-trapped a wood rat (pack rat) and several mice.

Although we prefer live traps, the catch has diminished to zero in recent weeks, but the devastation of the garden continues. So we've turned to an extermination technique that involves traditional spring-loaded mousetraps. This is a route we seldom pursue, but we've given the live traps plenty of time to produce results, and they've gone silent.

The previous week, with two spring-traps on the floating garden, we sat on our deck one evening, watching "second sunset" climb up nearby Goat Island. During summer, second sunset begins more than an hour after "first sunset" at our cabin, when we fall into the shade of the Bunster Range to the west. After that, the sun begins to set on Goat to our east, with the shadow of the Bunsters rising up from the water, climbing ever higher until it finally overtakes the entire towering slope of the tall island.

Watching the always-enchanting creep of the dark shadow up Goat, Margy suddenly yells out: "Oh! A robin is caught in the trap!"

Sure enough, a big robin has alighted on the floating garden, snapping the mousetrap. The beautiful bird is hopping around in a frantic flutter, dragging the wooden trap towards the edge of the water.

By the time I arrive at the garden, delayed slightly to grab a pair of gloves, the panic-stricken bird is in a sorry state. If you've never heard a robin scream, I can assure you it's an agonizing sound.

I try to sneak up on the robin from behind, but it sees me, and scoots ever-closer to the edge of the floating garden, where it may drag the trap into the water and drown. I try several different angles, and finally grab the bird just before it scurries off the float. Quickly, I lift the metal spring that's trapped the robin's leg. Immediately, the bird flies away, navigating quickly towards shore, bewildered but relatively safe.

The robin disappears into the bushes, and all is silent again. Margy and I are exhausted by the intense experience. As a minimum, the bird has experienced a broken leg. Will it survive, and will it be accepted by its mate? We've watched two distinct robins ever since the middle of spring, and we consider them part of our family.

"Let's get rid of the traps," says Margy.

"Of course," I reply.

There's no doubt about our action. We have erred, learned from our mistake, and want to quickly make restitution. I remove all of the traditional traps immediately, and set live-traps in their place, stilling feeling remorse over the poor robin.

The next morning, the robin reappears, flying competently, but landing a bit clumsily. Margy uses binoculars to inspect the awkwardly-hopping robin. Either one leg is missing, or it's retracted into the bird's thick-feathered belly. It has survived, and may even fully recover. We'll watch carefully over the next few weeks.

Now, on the morning of our departure for Rainbow Lodge, a day in advance of Tuesday's Canada Day, I load a wood rat and a mouse, live-trapped overnight, into the tin boat, to relocate them to nearby First Narrows, just as I've done so many times before. Maybe nature has acknowledged our return to live traps, and has filled them for us. Thus, the three of us (human, wood rat, and mouse) depart for our brief voyage. Big billowy cumulus clouds build upward, forming the foreground for a bright blue background. Summer is really here! And Canada Day, tomorrow, should be a warm, dry day. With wildlife relocation complete, it's time to pack up for a few days at Shermans Main.

* * * * *

AT 2 PM, WE MOTOR OUT OF HOLE IN THE WALL, with the tin boat tethered beside the barge. It's a bumpy start leaving the dock. When I shift into reverse to turn around and exit at the less-congested west entrance of the breakwater, a light crosswind pushes the barge to the side. In reverse, most boats (including this barge) hesitate in such turns due to the torque of the prop. Add a crosswind, and you may not turn at all unless you increase thrust. So we drift in the wrong direction as I try to turn around.

I change my mind, and decide to exit using the east entrance, but then I evaluate the width of this vessel with the tin boat rafted up to its side. Our Hewescraft is parked at this end of the cabin, and it will be a tight turn. No, this won't work either, so I change my mind again, I shift back into reverse, and begin to back out of the entrance behind me once again. In this boat, it's sometimes easier to back straight out than try to turn around, torque or no torque. Lesson learned – one of many.

Once we're outside the breakwater, I ask Margy to take the helm while I head to the bow with my red folding chair. It's the perfect day to retreat to my perch up front – a sunny last-day of June. In my chair, the breeze is a comfortable 7 knots, which equates to the speed of the barge. Slow and comfortable. I pull the flaps of my safari hat down over my ears, needing to protect myself from the sun for one of the first times this year. It's finally summer!

I stay up-front for most of the trip, walking back to the cab a few times to check that all is well with Margy. She enjoys driving this boat, and is content alone in the cab. Who would have guessed this (relatively) big boat would be a vessel she'd enjoy operating so much? We both are infatuated with the barge – easy to maneuver, getting out of our breakwater entrance excepted. And, more surprisingly, easy to off-load and on-load our quads.

Margy pulls in tight to the promontory where the Goat Island (Clover Main) dock is tucked in around the corner. We get a good look at the barge ramp and dock, empty today. According to the logging company office, traffic here is expected to increase later in the week, after the holiday passes, although it's an area where little road-building or logging has occurred recently. It's amazing how fast these dock locations fluctuate in their level of logging activity.

Farther north, past Olsen's Landing, is one of the most beautiful spots on this lake at the junction with Second Narrows. Today, stark-white scattered cumulus clouds seem to pour out of the snow-capped mountains to the north. Beartooth, with its distinct sharp-tooth peak, is my favourite. I've tried photographing this spectacular spot many times, but it can never be captured as perfect as you find it in person. Still, I pull out my camera and try again.

Approaching 2nd Narrows

We pull through Second Narrows and past the bay that holds Rainbow Lodge. Although there are no boats here today, the lodge looks amazingly well-kept. Everything is painted bright red, the docks look new, and the lawn recently mowed – not at all what I'd expected.

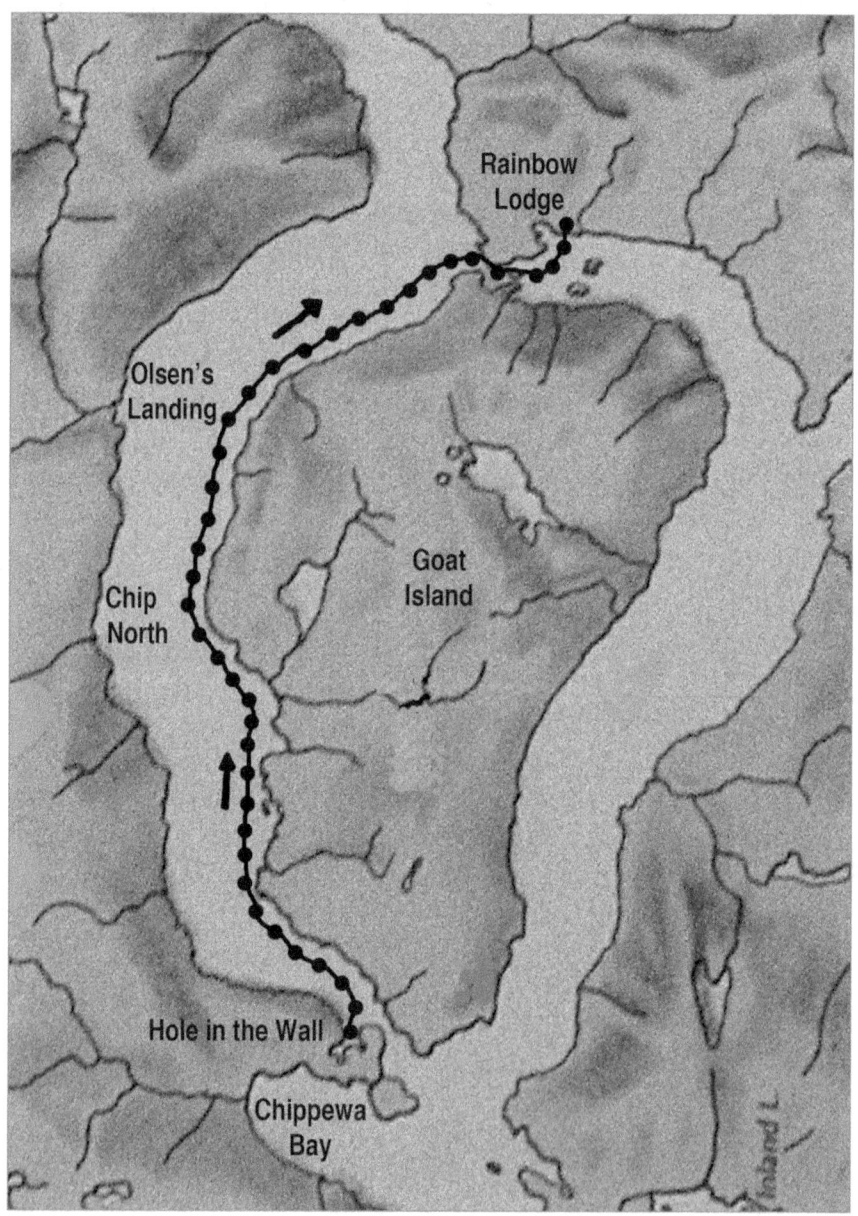

Canada Day (Shermans Main)

Just beyond the bay, the barge ramp looks fine except for a big log floating tight against shore right at the base of the ramp.

I let the barge drift toward shore, close-in and parallel to a rocky cliff on our left. I shift into neutral and flick the outboard motor's trim switch to raise the leg, making sure water is still pouring out of the cooling line. The depth sounder blares it's 6-foot alarm, and the vessel grounds itself in the shallow water less than a metre from the floating log. This will be an easy off-load, with our skookum metal ramps protruding well over the log as they extend towards shore.

The vessel's ramps hold us secure as I leisurely off-load the first quad, while Margy assures we stay parallel to the cliff by pushing her pike pole into the shallow bottom near our stern.

With our bikes now onshore, we motor over to the dock, and quickly convert the boat into our living quarters, with our tent pitched on the barge's deck and our temporary kitchen and living room on the dock. The sun beats down at a comfortable 22 degrees C, and it's a very pleasant place to be. So we decide to simply relax here rather than going riding today.

Barge Off-load at Shermans Main

Dock Campsite near Rainbow Lodge

On this Canada Day's eve, considerable boat traffic pulls through Second Narrows, as cabin owners travel to their retreats for the holiday. I picture the Shinglemill launch ramp as a beehive of activity tonight, always a fun place to watch boats launch on a holiday evening.

Our camping location feels secluded, since Rainbow Lodge is out of sight around the corner, and the nearby cabin on the other side of the dock is empty. Farther down along the wide eastward curve of the lake, a line of cabins stretches into the distance towards the next logging dock at Narrows. It's a peaceful, memorable night, with the warm, clear sky providing all the forecast needed for tomorrow, Canada Day.

* * * * *

THE NEXT MORNING, RAINBOW RIDGE TO THE EAST delays sunrise. Across the water, Goat Island's nearly-vertical granite cliffs are already bathed in bright sunlight. We're at the opposite end of the same Goat Island that forms our ever-present towering ridge adjacent to Hole in the Wall. It's contradictory, yet comforting, to visualize the vast extent of this massive island in the lake. I shouldn't be homesick less than

20 kilometres away from home as the crow flies, but I experience a perplexing sense of already missing my cabin on the lake.

Finally, well after 9 o'clock, we watch the sun break above the mountains, and the air begins to warm immediately. We listen to CBC Radio and then the local Powell River FM station, both filled with anecdotal stories about Canada Day. This is a true Canadian national holiday, and we're celebrating it in a wonderful location. But we should begin riding our quads soon to avoid traveling in the heat of the day.

We ride south first. I'm relieved to find that the "severely uphill" climb described by Rod must have been because he was hiking rather than riding. Margy has no problem with the first road we travel, tracking well above the shore on a wide newly-constructed logging road. I ride side-by-side to her right, since there's absolutely no road traffic here. On the downslope side of the main, I serve as a big red bumper between her and the precipitous downhill slope – her virtual guardrail. It seems to make her feel more comfortable. But when the main begins to climb more significantly, she slows and finally stops.

"Why don't you go on ahead, and I'll wait here," she says.

"Okay, take the bear spay," I say, handing the canister to her. "I wont' be gone long."

I know there's not much road left to the south, so I should be gone only a short while. But after traveling across the creek that marks the upper flow of Rainbow Falls into the lake below, I come to two trees across the main. At first, it looks like an intentional roadblock put here by Western Forest Products, so I plan to turn back. This a a no-chainsaw trip, as are most of our short journeys so far. I always carry large pruning sheers for branches, but seldom do I need a chainsaw. My attitude, generally, is that I'll seldom come to a blocked trail where a saw would easily get me through, so why bother carrying it? There are always other places to ride, so turning around is always an option. In extremely remote areas, however, a chainsaw can be an important safety tool in case a tree falls behind you, restricting your exit. This isn't one of those places. (Later, as I experience more problems without a chainsaw, I change my attitude.)

Besides, if the forestry company doesn't want me to proceed, I should turn around. But wait, is this really a deliberate barrier? The first (and largest tree) across the road is uprooted at the uphill end, so it fell into this position rather than being placed here by humans, and I can barely navigate under it on its higher end. The second (8-inch) diameter log does look intentionally placed behind the bigger log, but maybe not. And at one side of the road, the smaller log is wedged into the dirt, and I may be able to cross it on my quad. If the logging company did this on their own, it was a mighty sloppy job, which isn't the way Western Forest Products operates. So I give it a try, driving under the big log, and trying to drive over the small trunk at the side of the road where it's jammed into the dirt. But I get stuck.

Since I'm in four-wheel drive, my front wheels go successfully over the trunk crammed in the dirt, but my quad's undercarriage hangs up on the log. I can feel my bike tittering on the balance between its front and rear wheels. My wheels spin, so I stop before I make the situation worse. It's a long walk back to where Margy is parked. An example of why I should always carry my chainsaw, of course.

I manage to rock my quad enough to slide it back onto the rear tires. Once my bike has a solid footing, I'm able to back out over the log. But I don't give up. If I'm going to get stuck, I might as well get really stuck.

The small log is light enough that I can budge it at one end (which extends awkwardly out over the steep ledge on the side of the road). Being careful with my footing – getting stuck can be enjoyably challenging, but there's no need to take it to the extreme – I wiggle the log enough to shift it a few metres, where a thinner portion of the trunk contacts the road. I slowly drive over it in four-wheel drive. No problem!

Within another klick, I drive below a towering wall of freshly-cut granite on the uphill side of the road. This is an extensive area where blasting took more than the usual heavy-duty effort that accompanies road-building in this region. Maybe the logging company was concerned with people riding through this potential rock slide area, and that's why they blocked the road behind me – that is, *if* they (rather than nature) blocked the road.

Beyond this spot, I'm not able to go much farther before the road ends abruptly in a small slash. Turning around, I find a higher spur that's fun to climb, but it too ends after less than a kilometre.

When I finally get back to Margy's parking spot, she doesn't question why I've taken so long. Instead, she's walking along the side of the road near her quad, photographing berries and wildflowers.

Retracing our path back towards the dock, we pass though a ravine where huge rocks are strewn on both sides of the road. These are obviously massive "erratic" boulders dropped here by a retreating glacier. Seldom do you see such direct evidence of glaciation in this area. Yet 10,000 years ago, Powell Lake was a major u-shaped glaciated valley of ice that was melting, with the land starting to rebound upward from the reduced weight. This would form a cut-off oceanic fjord, and then eventually the freshwater lake that exists today.

We continue back towards the barge ramp, stopping only occasionally in shady spots to get out of the hot sun. While underway, the airflow counteracts the heat, and we're anxious to continue. We want to see the more northerly stretches of Shermans Main where logging was conducted a long time ago, and the vistas are even more spectacular.

Erratic Boulders along Shermans Main

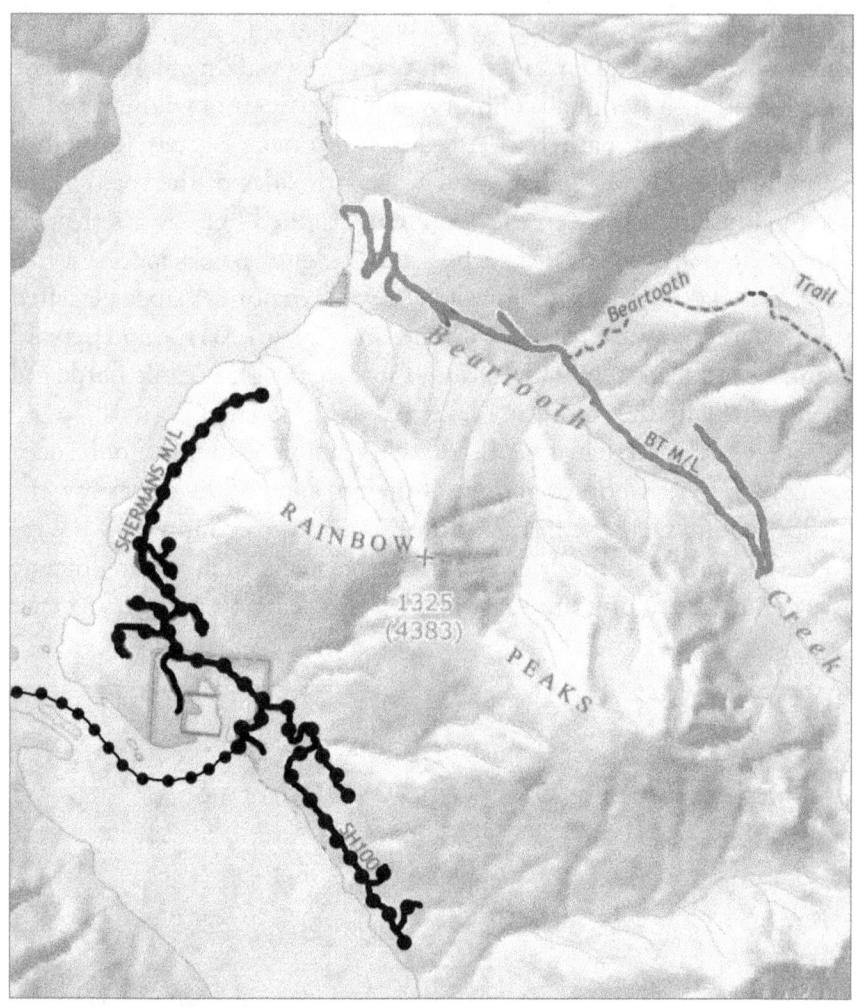

Canada Day at Shermans Main

Margy leads, and I'm surprised when she selects the higher road at a "Y," and then an even-higher spur at the next intersection. She feels more comfortable climbing here, although the drop-off to the side is still significant. However, because this is an older road, there's more roadside growth to cover the plunging downward views.

We're treated to magnificent vistas of the snow-capped mountains to the north, several of them with year-round glaciers. The views of Beartooth and other magnificent peaks is well worth the effort, but we can't ride far enough north to reach Beartooth Valley before Shermans Main ends. Maybe we can try the logging dock at Beartooth sometime soon. I've heard the main is completely overgrown, but it would be worth a look, and maybe we could walk up the old road a short distance. I fondly recall my first visit there years ago with John on motorbikes (*Up the Main*, Chapter 20). Beartooth Valley is on my list of top favourites.

On the highest road we ride today, I catch a glimpse of a horizontal vein of white granite on a wide, tall ridge to the north. It reminds me of "Slab Rock" near the upper-reaches of Falls Main. I first saw it during the trip John and I took to the head of Powell Lake several years ago (*Beyond the Main*, Chapter 2). That's a long ways away, but it's to the north, so maybe it really is Slab Rock. For a moment, I reflect back to that wonderful trip, and I imagine Margy and me riding at the Head, maybe later this year. With our barge becoming a comfortable mode of travel, this is a dream that's more than possible. It's gonna' happen.

Chapter 4

New Road in the Forest
Chippewa South

When I check in with Stuart at Western Forest Products, he always has a good handle on where logging is active and what mains are affected. But he often adds a precaution about road-building activity, since these operations are subcontracted to other vendors, and Stuart warns me they work using their own calendar. He often adds something like: "They're road-building on the east end of Dunn Main, but I don't know their schedule. So be careful with that."

Care around road-building is wise for a variety of reasons. The obvious is that this can easily close mainlines, and the dangers of dynamite makes it worth paying close attention. Additionally, on mains associated with Powell Lake barge ramps, road construction implies vehicles moving back and forth on the logging roads and at the barge ramps and docks that Margy and I use. In such locations, unlike the typical mains used by riders from town, loggers and road builders aren't expecting much quad activity. In contrast, on Goat Main (that's also an active recreational road), commercial drivers are always looking for opposing traffic. On these mains, busy with quads and other recreational traffic on weekends, logging or road-building movements can be expected to include pilot cars to lead the way, which improves safety. Procedures are technically the same on the mains accessed via Powell Lake, but I wouldn't count on seeing a pilot car on these roads.

Road-building fascinates me. In recent months, as a resident of the lake, I've heard the sound of dynamite reverberating through

Hole in the Wall during infrastructure construction at the new main at Chippewa South. In just a few weeks, the level of activity has mushroomed. *Road Cruise*, the most active road-building crew boat on the lake, is making regular trips between the Shinglemill and Chip South. I've seen this boat ply the waters of Powell Lake for years, always easily identified from a distance by its bright yellow colour.

Margy and I often usually travel to town along the east side of the lower lake. From there, near Cassiar Island, we look across to the west side where boats can be seen at the new logging dock at Chip South. Lately, *Road Cruise* and another boat or two are parked there, indicative of intense road-building activity. Since we're interested in what's going on, we sometimes return home to Hole in Wall by cruising along the west side of the lake, right past the new dock and barge ramp.

We sometimes stop and inspect the alterations visible in the staging area at Chip South. With the dock and ramp now complete, the primary change involves a variety of support equipment parked nearby – excavating equipment, dump trucks, water trucks, a fuel truck. Recently, a skid for dumping future harvested logs into the lake has appeared, an indication the road-building process may be approaching completion.

"I wonder if there'll be a break between completion of the roads and when they start logging?" asks Margy one day, as we bob in our boat next to Chip South's new dock, our engine at idle.

"I doubt it," I reply. "Time is money, you know. I bet they get busy logging as soon as the roads are ready."

We're both hinting at an idea that has formed within us nearly simultaneously. Great minds think alike! We've watched the new mainline advance steadily southward each week since construction began a few months ago. You can see intermittent traces of the new road between breaks in the trees. Chip South is becoming a more-elaborate logging site than we expected.

I'm not surprised when Margy states the obvious: "It would be exciting to see the new route before they go in and cut down the trees."

"Wouldn't that be something," I reply. "Brand-new roads through groves of big standing trees. If we could time things right, it'd be worth trying to ride it."

But coordinating anything involving road-building is difficult. They operate on their own schedule. Then again, they don't normally work on weekends, so we could use the new barge ramp then. If we wait too long, the place will be bustling with logging vehicles, and the beauty of a silent forest split open by a new road will be gone. If we're going to do this, we shouldn't wait.

* * * * *

An early July rain interrupts the beginning of summer. A significant storm moves in on Friday and runs rampant for two days, finally beginning to diminish on Sunday morning. The precipitation has become showery, and the forecast is for clearing in the afternoon.

When bright patches, not yet blue, appear to the south, we load up the barge with what we'll need for a day-trip to Chip South. Our plan is to ride the new mains, and then continue south to the Shinglemill to refuel the barge and a variety of portable containers we use at the cabin. I gas up the barge and quads from cans quite often these days. In fact, I recently made a trip to Canadian Tire just to add to my lineup of gas containers. Our home, John's Cabin Number 3, has become a growing marina of boats of various types, as well as an impromptu floating gas station.

After visiting the Shinglemill's pumps, we plan to stop at Haywire Bay on the way home, to visit our friends, Dave and Marg, who are camping there this weekend. Originally, we had planned to use our tin boat for the trip to Haywire, but why not visit our friends in the barge instead? Heck, we'll be in the neighborhood.

"We're neither sugar nor salt," I say to Margy as we step aboard the barge in a minor shower that reminds us the storm hasn't yet passed. It's one of my mother's sayings that I remember from growing up in the rainy climate of the Northeast U.S. As she used to say: "You're not going to dissolve when you get wet – you're neither sugar nor salt"

"Your mom probably never set foot on a barge," replies Margy, recognizing my popular saying. "But I guess she spent a lot of time in the rain."

By the time we're motoring south through First Narrows, the rain has stopped, and I actually see blue patches to the south. We carry rain gear in our quads, just in case. This trip will be short, and we're prepared for the instability expected in today's weather.

Margy drives as we angle towards Chip South, diverting to the right of Cassiar Island towards the west shore of the lake. The new barge ramp sits behind a promontory that blocks our view of the dock from this angle. The new log dump is readily visible, but we can't see whether there are any boats at the dock today. Hoping for no activity, I step out onto the deck of the barge, preparing most of what needs to be done before we off-load. If we find someone at the dock, we'll skip our quad ride and head directly for the Shinglemill. Thus, I leave the straps on the bikes, and delay starting the quads to warm up their engines.

When we round the point and find no boats at the dock, we're quite close to shore. So I ask Margy to shift into neutral to give me some time to catch up with preparation for the off-load. Within a few minutes, we're ready to land, and we creep in slowly to the new barge ramp. What a reassurance it is to find that each off-load is even more comfortable than the last.

After removing our quads from the deck, I back the barge out, and then motor the short distance to the nearby dock. Margy meets me

Ready to Off-Load at Chip South

there to grab my lines, and soon everything is secured, and we're ready to explore.

We ride our quads over to the new log dump, right around the corner. The turnaround area with the rock retaining wall behind it

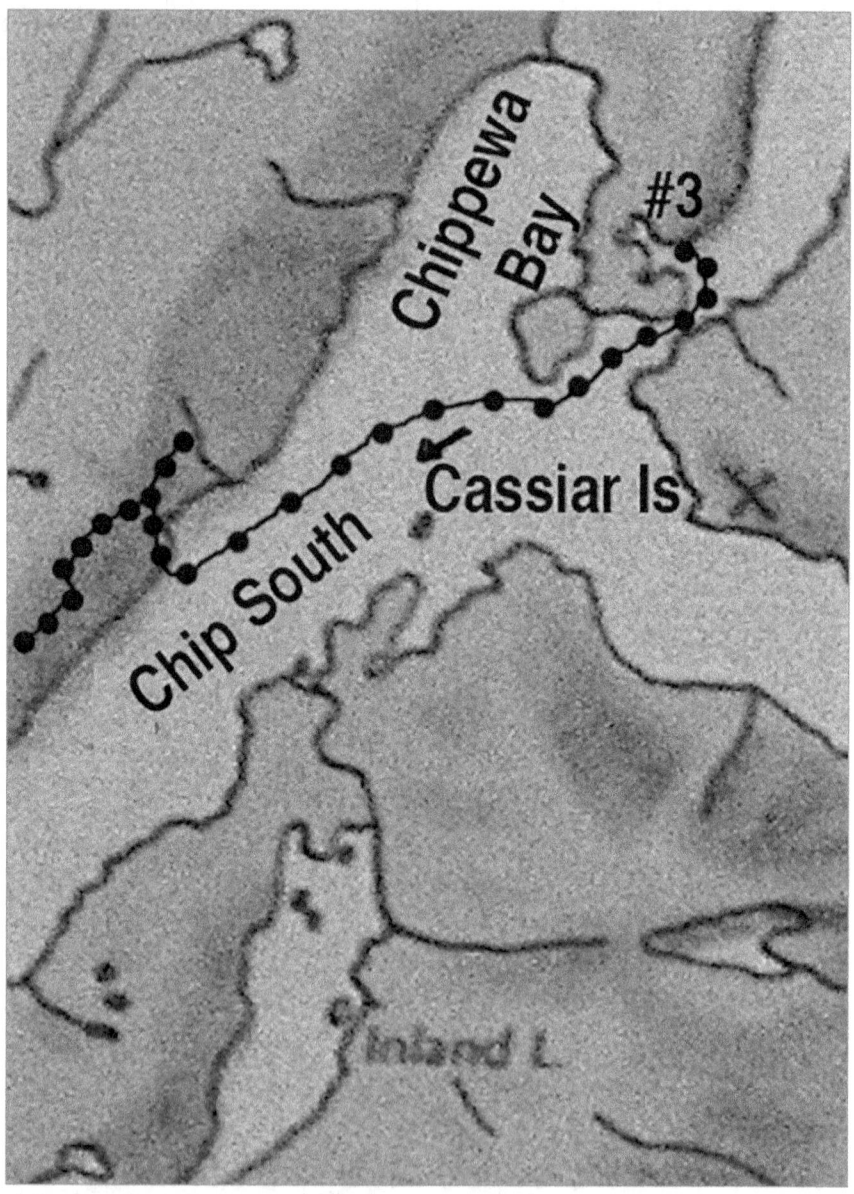

Trip to Chip South

are one of the most spacious I've seen on the lake. It's obvious that no shortcuts have been taken in construction at this new cut-block.

We first ride to the north, where the 1.5 kilometre road stops where a major stream is encountered. I've heard this main was originally intended to connect to Chippewa Bay's system of logging roads, but a bridge here would cost $100,000. A connection would be nice for both the logging company and off-road recreational riders, but I'd be surprised to see it in the near future. Often, new logging roads come oh-so-close to connecting with other older roads, but seldom actually join. Logging companies seem to prefer keeping new harvest areas separate from older ones.

We backtrack to the barge ramp, and continue upwards and south towards Powell River. This road goes farther than the northern spur, and it's a joy to ride through the nearly virgin forest. Of course, trees were cut down to make the road, and blasting was extensive on the rocky slopes, but it all looks so clean and tidy. Big logs lay alongside the new main, serving as guardrails in some places where the drop-off is precipitous. These logs have been stripped of their branches, and

Chip South's new Main

will be the first wood hauled out when the logging trucks make their initial runs on Chip South.

On the way back to the dock, we pause at several of the turnouts that have been prepared for logging vehicles. We look down through the openings in the trees to Powell Lake below.

As we navigate downhill, headed back to the barge, a light rain begins to fall, but not enough to cause us to stop and don our raingear. The ride has been short and sweet, and we're neither sugar nor salt.

Chapter 5

Looking for Spire Lake
Dunn and Spire Main, Goat Island

THE LUXURY OF KEEPING OUR QUADS aboard the barge at Hole in the Wall is the extravagance of flexibility. At a moment's notice, we can cast off for any destination on the lake. Since that includes access to extensive mainland destinations from the barge ramps at Fiddlehead Farm, Goat Lake, and Olsen's Landing, Margy and I are thrilled at our increased opportunity to ride our quads nearly anywhere in the local area. Add to that a chance to spend the night in a tent, one of our favourite pastimes. The barge project is a huge success.

When we came up with the idea of making the barge deck the permanent home for our quads, we received a variety of questioning looks from friends. I could read their stares: "Have you really thought this through?" their eyes said. As a matter of fact, Margy and I talked about this extensively before we purchased the barge. We're sure about our barge project – not so the people around us.

One of the first big tests of the lasting nature of this always-aboard setup comes when Doug arranges a date for use of the barge to haul construction materials to his cabin. To be truthful, one reason to keep our quads permanently on the barge is to easily fend off requests from friends who want to use it for transportation tasks. I'm sure it sounds selfish, but I didn't purchase this barge to improve up my good-guy image on the lake. (That's a joke, in case you don't understand my sense of humour – it's difficult to imagine any American attaining or maintaining a good-guy image on this lake, but we try.)

A barge is a valuable commodity around here, since everything that goes to cabins on the lake must go by water. For major construction projects, everyone would love to have access to a barge. I don't want to sound uncooperative, but my preference is to keep this boat as an easily accessible home for two quads. (Okay, I want to sound uncooperative.)

But when Doug hints he'd like to use the barge for hauling construction materials to his cabin, I'm quick to encourage him to establish a date that works for him. In fact, I insist on it. Doug is a sincere friend who I've trusted with the keys to my condo in Bellingham on various occasions when I've been in Canada, access to my boat on the chuck, and equipment privileges usually reserved only for John. Besides, if it weren't for Doug, I would never have found this barge. While searching online sources for a landing craft, it was Doug (boat buying scout extraordinaire) who led me to the Craigslist post advertising the barge. The seller didn't use the words "landing craft" anywhere in his online blurb, so my Internet search never found this boat, until Doug emailed me the link. As soon as I saw the photos, I was ready to buy the boat listed as a "barge. Thus, I'm pleased to help with Doug's transport project involving lumber, bags of cement, furniture, and the extensive odds-and-ends involved in a cabin construction project. I've learned how to load and unload the quads efficiently, so clearing the deck for cargo should be quick and easy.

Which proved to be exactly the case. Early one morning, I pull into Kinsman's Beach adjacent to the Shinglemill, off-load both quads, and chain them to a nearby metal post. Doug arrives a few minutes later with a trailer full of construction materials (plus a very full truck-bed), and we're ready to load. Fortunately, Doug brought his friend, Jeff, to assist, so I felt comfortable sending them on their way to Doug's cabin without me to help off-load. I spend the day in town catching up on errands, while Doug and Jeff take care of barge-hauling duties. Doug is thrilled, I'm thrilled, and Jeff learns his lesson about volunteering. Meanwhile, the barge proves its value to transport cabin materials.

* * * * *

During our first year with the barge, BC Day weekend is set aside for a long-awaited trip to the Head with John, but extremely hot temperatures are in the forecast. This was supposed to be a follow-up to the original pushed-raft journey John and I enjoyed two years earlier (*Beyond the Main*, Chapters 1 and 2). Our plans involve Margy, John, and I (Bro, too, of course) departing on Friday night.

As the weekend approaches, things change, as they often do. We could still make the trip, but the heat looks oppressive. The beauty of our always-ready barge provides numerous alternatives. The trip to the Head can be delayed until the weather cools off, since the quads will be ready to go when this hot spell is past. So we cancel our trip, but when things change even further (as is also often the case), Margy and I find ourselves at our float cabin on Sunday of the three-day weekend. With an additional day (Monday) available for riding almost anywhere, due to the shutdown of logging for the holiday, we consider a no-advance-preparation-needed trip to Goat Island. With extensive road-building now complete on a new spur of Dunn Main, logging and hauling is about to begin. But before the main is tied up, we have one last chance to ride the web of roads leading up from the Dunn Dock on the south side of Goat Island.

Just before 3 o'clock on Sunday, we're underway in the barge, with clear skies and an uncomfortable temperature of 27 degrees C. Conditions are perfect for a trip like this, although riding quads in the heat will be a minor disadvantage. If we break our ride into an early evening segment and another the following morning, we should be able to beat the heat. Nights on the lake were expected to remain moderately cool for the next few days, perfect for camping.

The North Sea below First Narrows is choppier than expected, but well within our self-imposed limits for the barge. With a west wind, the following sea makes the trip to the Dunn Dock go by quick. We're traveling along the south shore of Goat Island when we pass abeam Doug's cabin on the opposite side of the lake. I blast a prolonged honk of our horn.

"I can see Doug's boat in the binoculars," I say. "But it's probably too far for him to hear the horn."

"He's busy mixing cement, I bet," responds Margy. "He hauled enough of it with the barge to last a long time."

"Not for Doug. He's already looking for more."

While Margy drives, I go out on the deck to prepare the quads for off-load, but I complete only half of the tasks.

"I'm gonna' wait until we're sure there's nobody at the dock," I say to Margy when I return to the cab. "If there's somebody there, we can turn around and go home."

"The dock's big enough for several boats," she replies. "But I suppose someone might be parked at the ramp."

It's an unlikely situation, even though this might be a busy holiday weekend at the logging docks all around the lake. Off-road vehicles seldom use the lake's barge ramps, although there are a few local landing craft and barges that could handle the task.

When we round the point, the log boom pops into view, followed by the dock. At first, we think we see a boat.

"Might be Joel's houseboat," says Margy.

"Could be. But isn't it tied to the boom rather than the dock?"

"You're right," she replies. "And I think it's a green floating winch rather than a boat."

"I'm going out to finish up on the deck," I say. "Just hover around out here until I'm done."

Our plan seems clear and well communicated. So I go about my final duties, unstrapping the quads. I fuss with a jammed strap, and then hop aboard each bike to start the engines so they can warm up. Now I go up to the bow to position the ramps as far forward as possible to make quicker work of pulling them to shore. My goal is to minimize excessive sideways drift in this rather strong breeze.

When I reach the bow and kneel down to move the metal ramps, I look up and see the shore approaching a lot quicker than I expected. We're only 10 metres from the barge ramp, and closing fast.

"Whoa!" I exclaim, jumping up, and waving my arm towards Margy in the cab. "Back up!"

I doubt Margy can hear me from inside with the outboard motor running, but she understands my arm signal. I hear the motor clunk into reverse and rev up. We slowly back away from the shore.

When I finish repositioning the metal ramps and get back to the cab, Margy is in forward gear, completing a 360-degree turn to keep the barge in position offshore. It's too windy to simply shift into idle and maintain our position, which accounts for why we got so close to shore.

"I was drifting too close, and was about to back away," she explains. "The wind's stronger than I thought."

"Man, I thought we had a failure to communicate," I explain. "When I saw how close to shore we were, I thought you were headed in."

It isn't often that Margy and I get our signals crossed. However, today the wind intervened to make things look more exciting than they were.

Margy rolls out of the 360, and heads in again, while I go back to the bow. We're in perfect position now, so I wave my arm again – this time towards shore. Margy takes us into the barge ramp for the second time, and lines up for a good landing.

Off-load at Dunn Dock

Except it's not perfect. When I extend the metal ramps, one of them rests squarely on a pile of steel cable, which makes the two ramps uneven, and a bit awkward for off-loading.

"We'll need to bring it back to shore again," I say as I slide the ramps back aboard the barge.

"Let me try moving us with the pike pole first," says Margy.

"We're too hard aground for that," I say, "But you can give it a try."

She's right, and I'm wrong. With a push on the pike pole from the stern, Margy shifts the boat enough to allow both ramps to rest solidly on the ground. The rest of the off-load is flawless.

* * * * *

THAT EVENING AT ABOUT 5:30 when the air is cooler, we begin our ride up Dunn Main from the dock. We immediately encounter a line of vehicles ready for the big hauling event later this week. We pass a diesel tanker, several big logging trucks with their trailers in "carry" position on the back, a water truck, and several rugged vehicles for purposes I can't identify. It looks like there's going to be major action right after the holiday weekend.

We plan to ride the lower route today, the recently lengthened spur off Dunn Main that extends down the south side of Goat Island. By the time we get to the turn-off to the new road, we've already climbed well above lake-level and past what may be the most difficult portion of these roads for Margy. Although much of this area is newly-constructed roads designed for the large logging trucks, denuded hillsides no longer block the view on the downhill side. This would usually be a problem for Margy, but today she navigates these roads without a problem.

In California, years ago, Margy met with a psychologist to try to conquer her fear of quad-heights (as opposed to fear of airplane-heights, which has never been a problem). The therapy sessions consisted mostly of field trips to Los Angeles shopping malls, where the patient and her therapist traveled up and down giant escalators. It seemed to reduce her quad fears, but just riding trails like this and making gradual progress might be just as good as escalator therapy, and whole lot cheaper.

Since we've just reached the turn-off for the new Dunn Main extension, but are already so high, we decide to forego the turn, and ride up to Spire Main instead.

"Want to try the high route?" I ask at the intersection where we've stopped.

"Why not?" she answers. "The tough part might be behind us already."

And it is, although I'm surprised she wants to climb even higher. We continue on the upper portion of the mainline from here, a road that eventually leads north to Clover Dock on the other side of the island. When we're near the middle of the island, we stop at the junction for Spire Main, which climbs west and even higher.

Since all of today's climbing activity is going so well, we mutually decide to head upward towards Spire Lake. Here at the intersection, I suggest to Margy that she lead, since she's in a better position to judge her personal limits than I am. Sometimes when I lead, she follows behind until she exceeds her comfort zone, and then it's difficult for her to turn around and descend.

Spire Lake isn't on my GPS map, but this route should lead us there, if we can climb high enough without being blocked by fallen trees. These upper roads show little evidence of off-road travel since there's little recreational riding on this island. Still, these old paths remain easily navigable, regardless of nature's attempt to reclaim them. Sometimes they narrow to the point that total blockage is expected a few metres ahead, but then they widen again and are entirely open. Which is a good situation, considering I've left my chainsaw at home.

So far, on our barge trips, I've traveled without my chainsaw most of the time. My basic feeling is that I seldom come to a place where we're stopped by a fallen tree that could be removed easily, and if I am stopped, it's simple to just turn around and go somewhere else. But today I'll change my mind. Of course, there's a difference between learning by trial and error and obeying logic.

Today I learn my lesson when I try a side spur towards a goal that lingers in the back of my mind. At first, this high-altitude trail is wide open. And then there's a fallen tree. It's not a big tree, only about 8-inches in diameter, easily cut by a chainsaw. It angles across the trail, too high on the low end to drive across, and too low on the high end to drive under. With deep trenches on each side of the road, there's no way through. My chainsaw would have saved me with one brief cut. Yet we have to turn around.

Except, this is the rare case when I don't want to turn around. This route, according to my map, should lead to the old slash where "2-Trees" may reside. These big trees are part of my personal history on Powell Lake. From my home at Hole in the Wall, I can see two very big trees poke well above all of the rest on Goat Island. They rise from the very top of the ridgeline, as seen from my cabin deck, undoubtedly left on purpose by loggers of a much earlier decade. In my imagination, these loggers appreciated the grandeur of old-growth trees, and purposefully spared them from their saws. Also in my mind's eye, I believe they're in the old slash marked on my map.

The trail I'm now on – blocked by a single fallen tree – is a way to connect directly to the old slash, as least as I envision it. Of course, there could be hundreds of other fallen trees crossing the trail in front of me, but now I'll never know. More specifically, today I'll never know, for I'll need to come back. And for sure I'll bring a chainsaw.

Reluctantly, we turn around, maneuver back onto Spire Main, and continue to climb higher. After another kilometre, we encounter a spur to the right that might be an alternate route to the old slash and 2-Trees. But soon we encounter more trees that have fallen across the

2-Trees as seen from Hole in Wall (Telescopic View)

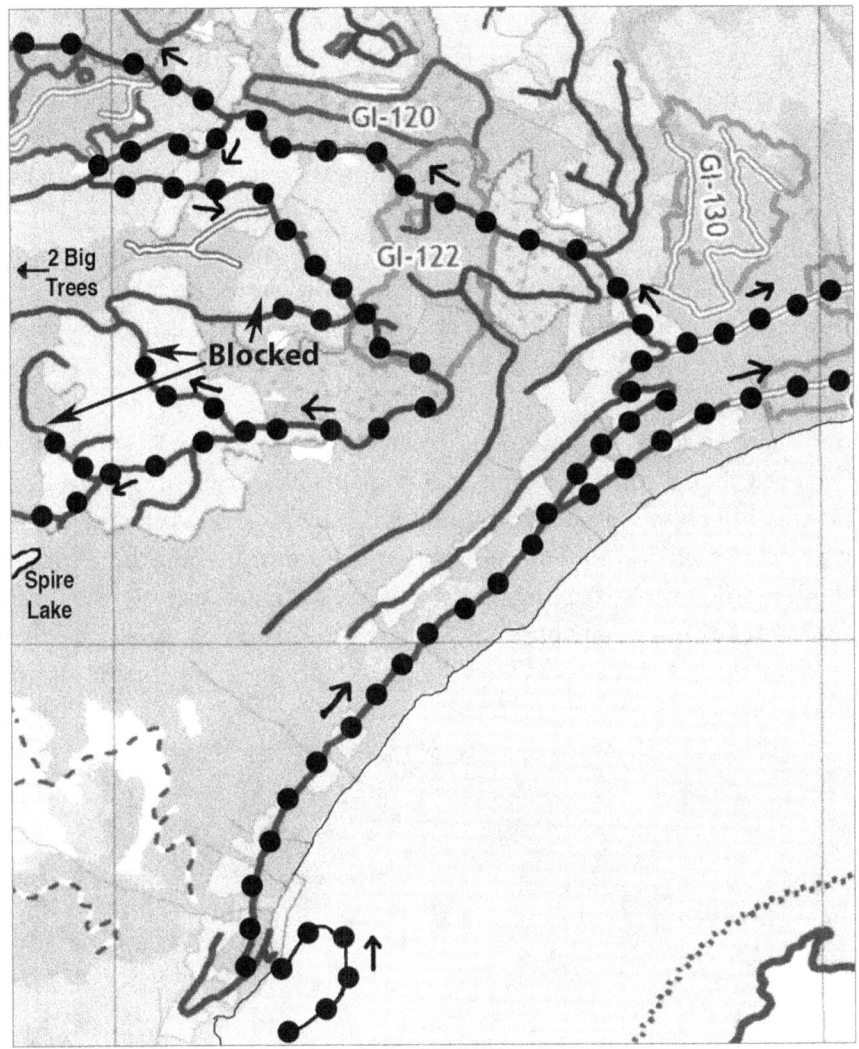

Looking for Spire Lake

trail. In this case, my chainsaw would have been of no help, unless it was joined by a dozen more saws. In front of us is a jumble of fallen trees extending as far as we can see. It's an avalanche of logs blocking the trail, impassible until someday loggers return to reopen the road.

There are other old spurs from Spire Main that would be worth exploring, but not tonight. Goat Island is a place Margy and I will want to return to often. We speak of Dunn Dock as a barge location for a "lifetime of riding." There's something special about the feel of these trails, comfortable and easier to ride than expected. The remoteness is accompanied by an aura of historic logging that still shows through, and we have it all to ourselves. (In our two days of riding from Dunn Dock on this holiday weekend, we never see another operating vehicle or any people.)

Spire Lake must be near, but we don't see it. We drive as far as we can go on the main, once again blocked by fallen logs, this time a jumble that's not quite an "avalanche." Looking up the road, more logs form obstacles, so a gaggle of chainsaws wouldn't make a dent. But we can walk this road, up and over the fallen logs, so we start hiking. After another kilometre, we can see down to Powell Lake, but we're looking directly into the setting sun, and the evening haze makes it difficult to identify landmarks.

Back at our quads, we pause for a snack of trail mix and juice on this lingering summer day. Then we start back down to the dock, past the connection to the newly constructed section, past the vehicles awaiting the big log-hauling event, and back to our barge. By the time we reach the dock, our headlights (always on when we ride, to make us more easily visible to other vehicles) finally have something to do in the oncoming twilight.

Barge Camping at Dunn Dock

That night, after eating dinner on the dock next to our barge, I look over the tracks laid on the GPS map, comparing them to the paper map in front of me. At the stopping point where we began our brief hike to look down on Powell Lake, Spire Lake was barely off to our left, and should have been easily visible. But we didn't see it. And the huge double trees seem to be located off to the north, just beyond the single fallen log that we couldn't cut. But we didn't see them either. We climbed all the way up Spire Main, missing both 2-Trees and Spire Lake.

We climb into our tent and watch lengthy holiday fireworks from a cabin across the lake. It's Sunday night – tomorrow is BC Day – and the lake is alive with boat activity, even after dark.

* * * * *

THE NEXT MORNING, we head back up the mainline to the same intersection where we turned uphill towards Spire Main. Now we turn right, along the new road, which extends east, high above the south shore of Goat Island. The views of Powell Lake below are spectacular – too spectacular for Margy. I ride parallel with her on the downhill side, acting as a human guardrail. It works for a while,

Giant Shovel on Dunn Main

but soon Margy hunches down in her seat, with her head almost below the handlebars, a sure indicator we're about to stop. When we do, it's beside a huge road-building shovel, left behind from the previous weeks.

"Why don't you stay here, and I'll go ahead a little ways," I say. "Won't be gone long."

"Sure," she says.

Just in case, although she'll be comfortable here in the shade of the giant shovel, I leave her with the bear spray. There's lots of bear scat on these roads, but so far we haven't seen any on this trip. Other than squirrels and birds, the island seems devoid of life, although we know it isn't.

I ride for only a few more kilometres before the new road comes to a sudden dead end, which surprises me. I'd hoped this new extension would connect with South Frogpond Main. I've ridden that road past the outlet from Frogpond, up and towards the now-extended Dunn Main. But the two roads don't connect.

Road Cruise near Head of Powell Lake

On the way back to the big shovel, I reflect on the road-construction process. Every time a logging road is built, it's a heavy-duty operation. I've watched crew boats go in and out of docks being used for road-building, and I've heard about the intensive construction process that includes exhaustive surveying and huge blasts of dynamite. *Road Cruise*, the aptly named crew boat, is my regular reminder of the marvels of road-building and the many jobs it creates for Canadians in this region.

When I rejoin Margy, we track back along the main to explore some of the new spurs that have been created in the road-building process. As we go higher, each spur is shorter, and all terminate in dead ends.

Then we turn back up the connector road to Clover Main and the dock on the other side of the island. We pass the turnoff that leads up to Spire Main, continuing down through wide strands of big second-growth trees that offer occasional scenic views towards Clover Dock to the north and the big logging slash at Chippewa North across the lake.

As we approach the dock, there's an abundance of vehicles. Most are associated with logging operations, but some are trucks and SUVs used by hunters and the few locals who occupy float cabins at Frogpond. Since there are no boats at the dock today, that indicates there's possibly no one on huge Goat Island today except us.

After a lunch break at Clover Dock, we ride back up the road towards the Spire Main turnoff, determined to try again to find Spire Lake and maybe even 2-Trees. We climb the old main, and I watch closely for any deactivated spurs that turn off to the right. The first one is the path I know is blocked by a fallen tree. Nevertheless, I make the turn, and we soon come to a stop at the problematic log.

I get off my bike, and try putting my full weight on the high side of the log, jostling it back and forth, and hoping to break it. Maybe this would work on an old fallen log, but it's far too fresh today. I ask Margy to join me, adding her weight to the task. Nothing.

In a futile attempt to do something, I employ a pair of pruning sheers I always carry with me on my quad. Of course, the sheers won't remove this log, but I pound with the cutting edge, making a tiny dent in the log. Maybe with a few hundred hours of grinding by hand with this puny blade, I could finally cut through. It's obviously a hopeless task.

"Next time," I say to Margy. "2-Trees is right over there."

She knows what I mean. Next time I'll bring my chainsaw. And there definitely will be a next time.

"Do you want to try to walk it," she asks.

"Too far, and it's too hot. Besides, the road is probably totally blocked farther along. But if I had my chainsaw, we could at least give it a try."

"Next time," she repeats to me.

We return to Spire Main, and farther up the road arrive at an intersection that beckoned to me last night when it was too late to try any more spurs. This road leads to the left, and might give us a view of Spire Lake. But it doesn't. Instead, the road descends and increases in width, indicating it might connect with the road that leads down to Dunn Dock. In fact, that's exactly the case, and we're able to descend all the way back to the barge.

Two trips up Spire Main with two aspirations – find Spire Lake and reach 2-Trees. Neither goal is accomplished this weekend. But we'll be back to try again, and that trip will certainly include the elusive goal of 2-Trees. And next time, I'll bring my chainsaw.

Chapter 6

Old Haunts
Fiddlehead Farm and a Myraid of Lakes

OUR FIRST SUMMER OF BARGE OPERATIONS on Powell Lake is drawing to a close. September days are growing shorter, which means longer and colder nights in our tent on the barge. This could be the last overnighter, so where will we go?

The Head, of course, still looms in my imagination. But when I phone Stuart, he warns me against the trip, since they're hauling on weekends now. We'd be able to ride Daniels Main, but the roads to the southeast (Jim Brown, Falls, and Cypress Main) will be off limits because of the hauling route. This is a destination better left until next year.

Except for our trip to Goat Lake early in the summer, it's been years since I've ridden the roads frequented by the Powell River ATV Club. Thus, the allure of Fiddlehead, especially with little hauling in the area. If we stay west of Goat Main, we shouldn't encounter any logging vehicles. However, an in-town Saturday full of college football television takes precedence (as it always does during September), but we could depart on Sunday, ride that afternoon, camp overnight, and ride again on Monday. Weekdays are normally a problem due to logging in this area, but a phone call to Western Forest Products determines the log hauling areas are well to the south of Fiddlehead. Although ATV riders from Powell River will have restricted access, logging in our location in the north will be quiet all the way down to Haslam Lake. That's a lot of room for exploring.

On Sunday, September 8th, Margy and I depart Hole in the Wall right after noon, with a high temperature forecast of 25 degrees. As is typical when departing the Hole in summerlike conditions, calm water quickly turns to medium-sized waves in the North Sea below First Narrows. The barge handles these conditions well, water splashing harmlessly over our bow, but it's always surprising to encounter conditions that change so fast.

I navigate towards Pickle Point, planning to swing close enough to the old barge ramp to evaluate its suitability for off-loading sometime soon. We surveyed this spot a few weeks ago, and it was shocking to see how overgrown the ramp area has become. But maybe a closer second look will provide a different impression. After all, a chainsaw can clear a trail quickly, as long as the obstacles don't go on forever.

"Not many places to ride," says Margy, as we get a little closer, with a better view of the upper logging road.

"Never was," I reply. "It's amazing it was profitable to establish a logging operation here for so little acreage."

I remember this site when it was active. This was a quick in-and-out by the logging company, with road spurs only a few klicks in length. Although there's not much to see now, it would be nice to add it to our already-accumulating list of ramp-access conquests. I'm guessing that Beartooth Main, once a bustling logging road that John and I explored with our motorbikes, has fallen into this same state – too overgrown to ride. Beartooth would be a major loss. Pickle Point, not so much.

As we approach the headland, I slow to idle. We slip past the barge ramp, only 10 metres from shore, getting a good look at the extent to which nature has overtaken the road. Right at the water's edge, a large alder grows in the center of the ramp. Farther back, I can see a line of alders stretching well uphill until the road disappears into the bigger trees.

"Even a chainsaw would have a battle here," I say to Margy. "That first tree isn't the only obstacle."

"Not worth the effort," she replies.

Continuing down the south shore of the lake towards Fiddlehead, we round the point near Doug's cabin. Coming around the corner, we find his boat at the dock, with another tied next to it.

Honk! Honk! I toot the horn to announce our sudden arrival, and almost immediately Doug appears on the deck overlooking his cove, waving and motioning us towards the dock. His brother, Malcolm, is here, too. That accounts for the second boat. Doug has been upgrading the structures surrounding the cabin, leaving the living quarters – the biggest challenge of all – until last.

With two boats already tied to his dock, there's no room for our barge. No problem – we just want to say hello. I shift into neutral, and drift a few feet away from Doug, who is now joined by Malcolm. Margy and I yell greetings across the short stretch of water. Malcolm grabs the rail of our barge, and we sit this way as we catch up on Doug's construction news. Then we explain our trip to Fiddlehead.

"I hear they're logging at the head of Haslam," says Doug. "So be careful there tomorrow. It's a weekday, you know."

"We figure we can still ride north of Haslam tomorrow," I say. "Maybe we'll just stay on Rainbow Main or go down to Giovanno."

"Should work," replies Doug. "Have fun!"

With that, we're off again, slipping along the shoreline towards Fiddlehead Dock.

* * * * *

A HALF-HOUR LATER, we're approaching the Fiddlehead barge ramp in nearly calm conditions. Margy steers us towards shore, raising the motor for the last few metres as a precaution. But the lake's low water level this time of year results in a steeper-than-normal ramp upslope, providing lots of buffer for our prop. She keeps the motor running as we off-load.

I drive the quads to shore, and then hop back onto the barge's bow as Margy backs our boat away from the ramp. She maneuvers to the nearby dock, which is riding crooked in the water after several years of almost no use by the logging company. Still, it's a good place to park the barge.

Before we go riding, we set up our tent on the boat's deck. Usually, after returning from a ride, we're tired, and the minimal effort to raise a tent seems daunting. So we take the time now, including inflating our air mattresses and getting our sleeping bags and overnight gear prepared. It takes only a half-hour to construct our temporary home

Camping at Fiddlehead Dock

and ready the adjacent area on the dock as our lounge and dining room. We're used to being the only boat at the dock in locations like this, and today is no exception. So we're spoiled once again, spreading our gear out as if we own the dock; yet we make sure there's room for someone else, if they arrive while we're riding.

This logging dock is one of the few we've encountered with a cabin adjacent, and this nearby floating cabin looks inhabited. The curtains are open, but no one is visible, and no boat is tied to the deck.

"Might be gone on a boat ride," says Margy, motioning to the cabin. "I bet they'll be back soon."

This is Sunday, and even though Labour Day has passed (a day when recreational activity on the lake seems to suddenly stop), there's quite a bit of boat traffic today, with lots of cabins occupied. But even if someone is here, they probably won't stay overnight, since tomorrow is a workday. I'm hoping we'll have privacy tonight.

As if on cue, a small runabout approaches, heading straight for us. As the boat slows, I wave, and the woman in the passenger seat waves back, followed by a big swing of the arm from the little girl in the back seat. The driver cuts power, and the boat immediately comes down off plane, and maneuvers towards the nearby cabin. After experiencing so much solitude on this lake, this suddenly seems somewhat like urban living.

A few minutes later, Margy and I are on our quads, headed for Fiddlehead Farm. It's a place steeped in local history involving commune living and (more recently) wilderness tourism (*Farther Up the Main*, Chapter 6). Ten years ago, there were old abandoned buildings to explore on this farm, but now nothing remains except a single shed (rejuvenated by the ATV Club) and an old apple orchard.

On the short drive to the deserted farm, less than a klick, we navigate through several intersections where Rainbow Main, Giovanno Main, and several unnamed roads cross. Right away, this feels different from the other areas we've been riding in recent months. At most barge ramps on the lake, a single main leads up from the shore. Although the roads typically split into logging spurs, there's seldom a need for extensive knowledge of the layout, and a map would be unnecessary. Here we find dirt roads everywhere, intersecting and heading off in different directions with little or no signage. Those who ride here, including the Powell River ATV Club, know where they're going, and take it all in stride. To me, it's a hodgepodge of mains and trails that makes me feel disoriented.

When I rode here a decade ago, I simply followed John, so I didn't need to know where I was going. John served as my infallible map. Today, however, I don't like the feeling of not knowing exactly where I am, although my GPS track always stands ready to lead me back to the barge if I become lost. When in doubt, simply following the squiggly black line.

At the Fiddlehead orchard, Margy gathers some of the fallen apples from the ground, tart but still fresh: "I wonder why the bears haven't gotten these already?" she asks.

"Plenty of bears this year," I add, since we've already seen more than the normal number on our summer rides. But for some reason, they've left apples on the ground at one of their well-known spots.

Fiddlehead Farm Apple Orchard

From here, a sign on a tree points the way to Giovanno Main. This will take us south to Giovanno Lake and then Haslam. The plethora of roads in this area is amazing. Without signage, the location of the myriad of nearby lakes tend to merge in my mind. The size and shape of these lakes usually give them away on our printed map, but looking at them through the trees along a main can be deceiving. And to check a map while driving a quad is nearly impossible. Thus, here I am in one of the least remote sections I've driven in months, with minimal sense of my exact location.

At first, all goes well, with Giovanno Lake appearing on our right, precisely how I remember it. Margy's sense of location is generally better than mine, so when I pull up next to her where she's stopped, she says: "That's the trail to Poki's Place."

She's right, and now I can picture it – a winding trail down to Giovanno Lake. A few hundred metres later, Margy stops again beside a nondescript trail nearly hidden in the bushes: "Marg's Manor," she says. Right again, and it's easy to visualize once she identifies it.

Farther down Giovanno Main, we deviate north towards Tin Hat Mountain, a route Margy has never ridden all the way. John and I once drove to the end-of-trail parking area at Tin Hat, and followed the short hiking trail up the final stretch to the mountaintop. Margy and I later started up the route to Tin Hat, but stopped short when Margy became uncomfortable with the drop-off to the side. Maybe the route has been altered in the intervening years, or Margy's increased tolerance for precipitous slopes may make today's climb easier. Good thoughts, but it's not to be.

Although the trail is well groomed, Margy begins to feel uncomfortable almost right away, and I encourage her to turn around before it becomes a problem. There are always lots of other places to ride. Together, Margy and I navigate a lot of sublime paths, and there's no need for her to attempt a trail that makes her feel uncomfortable. As for me, I'm just glad to be out and about on my quad, and where I ride is almost inconsequential.

So we start back downhill towards Lewis Lake, a good destination for a rest stop. However, somehow we make the wrong turn – once again the preponderance of unmarked intersections conspires against us. Unknowingly, we're headed down the east side of Lewis Lake, and the entrance to the camping area is on the other side. After recognizing our error, we decide to continue all the way to the intersection with Spring Main (which is well marked). At that junction, sitting side-by-side on our quads with darkness approaching, we elect to reverse our course and continue back up the hill. Maybe we'll stop at the Lewis Lake campsite, if we can find the turnoff just below the lake.

Margy leads, stopping at an intersection that seems headed in the right direction, but we're not sure it leads to Lewis Lake.

"This might be the turn," I say to Margy as I catch up to her. "But I'm really not sure. In fact, I'm pretty frustrated by not knowing where I am today, so let's just continue back over the same route we came down. It'll get us back to the barge faster."

Margy is quick to agree, since she's more concerned about our available gas than I am about the approach of sunset. We start back up Lewis Main, again skirting the lake on the east shore where it's inaccessible. The good news is – for the moment, at least – we know exactly where we are. For both us, we're now simply happy to be traveling on our quads on a reasonably good road, enjoying the towering forest scenery.

For the return trip, as for most of the day, I ride next to Margy on the downslope side of the road, even in places where it's not essential

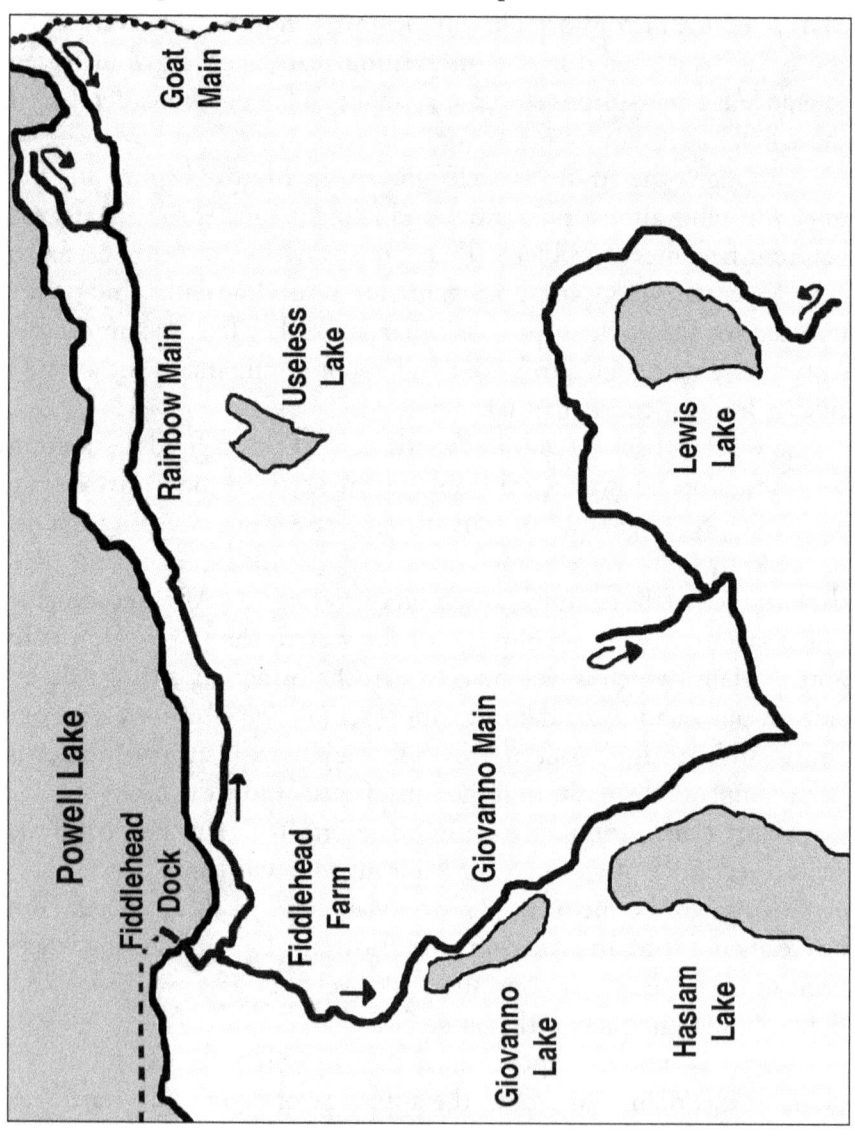

Fiddlehead Trip

for her comfort with the terrain. In this position, I'm out of the swirl of dust behind Margy's quad on the dry main.

However, I'm careful about on-coming vehicles. I recognize that I've become used to not needing to worry about approaching traffic on the remote roads we travel near Powell Lake's barge ramps. Today is different, with more vehicle activity in the area. Yet, I'm still surprised when we encounter a pickup truck on the way back to the barge. We meet on a wide curve, where I've just dropped behind Margy instead of riding the dust-free abeam position. I've returned to the right side of the road for the curve, and none too soon. Both the truck and our quads are traveling at slow speed, with lots of time to react. So it's not a near-miss, but it's a reminder to watch out for traffic on blind spots on the main. I wave to the truck, and he waves back, leaving me to ride the rest of the way with a bit more caution.

In fact, in another klick, we encounter a second pickup truck, and it's an even less-exciting confrontation. Although it's on a narrow section of road this time, we're both on our own side, and slow a bit further until we've safely past.

Although I've been somewhat disturbed by the "semi-lost" nature of most of today's trip, it's been a great ride, with some animal life thrown in. A large family of grouse and a lone fully-grown bear are encountered along the way, and that always makes the day more exciting – nature at its best. Which proves it's not where you go, but how you get there that counts.

Back at the barge, the nearby floating cabin is now secured for the night, with all of the curtains closed and the boat gone. We'll have the dock area to ourselves tonight. Except…

No sooner do we get our boots off than another small runabout is headed right towards us. At first it looks like the same boat we saw earlier, headed to the nearby cabin rather than our dock. But it doesn't deviate from heading straight towards us.

"Guess who?" says Margy. "It's John!"

No way. She kidding – what would John be doing in this part of Powell Lake today? Unless, of course, he's come here just to find us.

Sure enough, it's John, with Jimmy in the passenger seat. When they pull up to the dock, John is all smiles: "Found you!" he says.

Which shouldn't surprise me, considering how often John shows up when I least expect him. As I've noted many times – John is everywhere.

"Been fishing up at the Head," says John as I grab his bowline. "Decided to go home on the other side of Goat Island."

That explains Jimmy as his passenger, since he's one of the most enthusiastic fishermen I've ever met. Jimmy will go a long ways to find a trout.

What's more, Margy and I aren't the first quad riders he's purposefully met at a logging dock today. John's brother, Rick, rode into Olsen's Landing on Powell Lake from Theodosia, just to meet John at Olsen's dock. As is typical of John, he'll travel to extremes to meet people. So far this summer, while traveling with our quads on the barge, this is the second logging dock where I've met John, and I'll meet him at a third in another week. That's more than a mere coincidence.

John and Jimmy don't stay long, for darkness is approaching for them, too. The boat trip back to the Shinglemill will take over a half-hour from here. So off they go, all four of us waving and yelling. Make that five, counting Bro.

* * * * *

AFTER BREAKFAST ON THE DOCK the next morning, we decide to concentrate on Rainbow Main, which runs alongside Powell Lake all the way to the intersection with Goat Main. We can't travel beyond there today, since it's a Monday, and there's active hauling coming down from Dianne Main. Still, there's much to see between here and Goat Main.

I walk up the dock ramp to shore, planning to gas up our quads for today's ride. In the process of refueling, I break the plastic filler extension on the gas can (brittle – not my fault), but I complete the refueling without it. A few minutes later, back on the dock, I knock my red pair of reading glasses into the lake (of course, you have to drop them first, and then kick them in just the right direction) – my fault.

Meanwhile, Margy is packing up the tent, so while I'm kicking my glasses overboard, she manages to drop a tent support pole off the barge – her fault. To add to the continually deteriorating situation, I've also managed to lose my camera case (but not the camera) – again, my fault. I think I may have driven away on my quad yesterday with the case loose on top of my rear storage box. It's a back-to-back series of self-imposed bad luck, and not a good start to the day, particularly if you're superstitious.

Today, just getting onto nearby Rainbow Main from the barge is a bit of a challenge. Although the road practically terminates at Fiddlehead Dock, I closely check my map to try to determine which of the initial intersections is really Rainbow Main. I don't expect signage to be of any help, but according to my map, it's the second left turn departing the dock area. However, not all left turns are the same, since some of the spurs are big enough to look like old mains.

Margy leads, slows a bit at each of the intersections, but continues ahead until there's a fairly obvious main to the left. After we've traveled a short distance, it's obvious we're on Rainbow Main because it opens up a bit and we're traveling parallel to the shoreline, just as I remember it from years gone by.

Looking Down on Goat Lake from Rainbow Main

The ride to Goat Main goes without incident, regardless of the previous four-peat of dropped and broken objects. It's a good thing we're not superstitious. Rainbow Main is generally in good repair, although overgrown in sections. There are few turnoffs on either side, except for dead-end logging spurs, so we just keep going. Finally, we arrive at the intersection with Goat Main, where we stop, awaiting logging trucks barreling down the road from Dianne Main. None at the moment.

From here, we drive back on Rainbow Main only a short distance to an overlook near the entrance to Goat River. One of the few float cabins in Goat Lake forms the focal point for a majestic view, with Powell Lake in the distance beyond Goat River.

On the ride back to the barge, with Margy leading, she deviates to the right on an unmarked trail that heads towards Goat River. Recently pruned branches protrude into the old trail, and the path ends in a small clearing that's obviously very close to Goat River, although the river is hidden by the bushes. We find a walking trail to the water's edge (to someone's secret fishing spot), tightly encroached by thick brush and jutting berry vines. Rather than thrash to the river though "nature's barb wire," we turn around and return to the parking turnout. From here, we ride back to Rainbow Main, and then drive non-stop to the barge, after another enjoyable day of riding.

We pack up what remains of our gear, but as we're gathering our equipment on the barge, Margy sees something we missed earlier in the day. She notices the bright glint of a tent pole in 5 metres of water, right next to the barge. After at least a dozen tries, I finally retrieve the pole using a fishing lure. (A full week later, we return to the dock in our Hewescraft with an underwater observing tube and another jigging lure, locate my red reading glasses in the water near the dock, and recover them. A few days later, my camera case reappears inside my quad aft box when I'm hunting for a map, but the gas can filler extension never fixes itself.)

Now it's time to load the quads at the barge ramp. We're getting a lot better at this process, departing the ramp today with barely a hitch. In a few short months, we've become experts at quad loading and unloading, faster and more thoroughly than we'd expected. The barge is a joy to operate, maneuver, and dock – as easy as any boat I've ever owned.

Departing the Fiddlehead ramp, Margy drives towards the north shore of the lake (south edge of Goat Island) while I go through my secure-the-cargo actions – strap and chock the quads, fuel valves off, GPS secured, metal ramps stowed, storage containers inventoried, and everything prepared for the next trip.

Our destination is only a few klicks away, near the logging dock at Dunn Main. Just to the east, along the shore, is a place we've visited before when the lake level was low, but not in recent years. We remember exploring an old main that led inland from this spot, past a big overgrown-with-bushes logging winch. We think we can find it again, and we're interested in its condition. Powell Lake is nearly at its low water level extreme this month, and it's a good day to access the old logging road (if we can find it) from the beach.

We take the barge ashore near where we expect to find the old winch. The sandy beach makes for an easy landing, but we're unable to find the old main. I think I'm able to discern the road in the bushes,

Barge near Dunn Main Dock

vastly overgrown. Unfortunately, we're now dressed in shorts and water shoes, not the best attire to slog through the bush in rough terrain. Instead, our attention is quickly diverted by the condition of the beach at this wide, sandy spot, with its clear and warm water. The depth sounder in the barge registers a water temperature of 73 degrees (on the Fahrenheit scale), which is about as warm as we ever find it on this lake. Soon we're swimming near shore and then air-drying ourselves in the warm sunshine.

After departing our tropical beach getaway, we travel along the south side of Goat Island, using the thrust of the kicker to troll for trout. Margy fishes from the front of the barge, sitting on her quad – catching nothing, but delighted by the sunshine. The past two days conclude our last overnight barge trips for a summer I'll always remember as the best ever. (Until next summer, which is even sunnier, warmer, and more exciting.)

We troll slowly past Bob's floating cabin, Margy still fishing from the front. I drive the barge, with my fish pole protruding out of the

Margy Fishing from Quad

cab door. It's been a terrible year for catching trout on Powell Lake, but a wonderful summer of sun and adventure.

We round the corner into First Narrows. I turn off the kicker, and restart the main engine for the final leg of our journey. I make the left turn into Hole in the Wall, passing Max and Monica's floating cabin on the left, and then glide between the cabins jointly owned by Dave and Louie and the one that belongs to Jess. There's one more float cabin on the left – John's Number 2 – and then our wonderful floating home on the right that we call Number 3. We're home.

Chapter 7

Donkey Trail
Above Museum Main, Chippewa Bay

STEAM DONKEY SITES throughout coastal British Columbia have been preserved by loggers and off-road recreational enthusiasts. These museum-like locations of old logging equipment are favourite riding destinations for ATV riders from Powell River, including two donkey locations above Chippewa Bay.

Appropriately-named Museum Main leads upward from Chippewa, passing the first (more-easily accessible) steam donkey, continuing on to the second. Getting to these preserved treasures of logging equipment involves a challenging ride from town over the Bunsters Range on the rugged Last Chance Trail, and then down to Chippewa Bay via a lengthy series of wide switchbacks. From Chippewa, it's a substantial ride back upward on Museum Main to the steam donkeys.

Since the Last Chance Trail isn't suitable for inexperienced quad riders, the more common route to the donkeys is even longer. It involves a ride into Theodosia Valley from Southview Road, a lengthy trip up and over Heather Main, down to Chippewa Bay, and finally back up to the donkeys. By either route, it's a round-trip that can consume all the daylight of a long summer day.

John and his friends have been working to improve an old logging road high above Museum Main as an alternate and much quicker route to the steam donkeys. Once completed, quad riders will be able to access the historic equipment without descending all the way to Chippewa Bay. Plus, it will create a circle route to the bay below. Riders will be able to take the shorter route down (from the Last Chance Trail) and the more-lengthy route in the opposite direction, or they can reverse the course. Any ride is more enjoyable if you don't need to retrace your track going home.

But this old, overgrown logging road, a path John calls the Donkey Trail, is so deteriorated and choked that it has become completely impassable, even impossible to identify in some spots. Still, John and his friends have big plans. They'll open the old road running south from the Last Chance Trail, making it wide enough for a quad to navigate to a location less than a hundred metres above one of the old steam donkeys. Then they'll somehow figure out a way to drop down the remaining distance. As trail rebuilding goes, this will be a major project to span several seasons.

"You can meet me there," says John one morning over the phone. "If you want to help with the trail, I'll be there about 11 o'clock."

What he's implying is that I should use our barge to access a steep trail that leads up from Hole in the Wall, drive my quad to Chippewa Bay, and then and up the series of wide switchbacks leading to the base of the Last Chance Trail. We'll have the entire afternoon to work on the Donkey Trail.

Two problems – I've never used this steep trail from Hole in the Wall, and it's so precipitous that even John requires differential lockers to climb it. But there's an alternative that immediately enters my mind.

"Okay, I'll give it a try," I reply. "But if I'm not there by 11 o'clock, you'll know what happened to me – I chickened out."

I wait to see how John reacts to my statement involving the word "chicken," knowing he has a good sense of my limitations on a quad. I'm concerned about this trail from Hole in the Wall. It's a straight-shot upward without any switchbacks. I've walked this trail, and it seems near my limits on a quad.

"You'll definitely need your lockers, so be careful," adds John before he hangs up.

When John substitutes the word "careful" for "chicken," I know he's acknowledging that this trail may be beyond my limits. Which makes me ponder the alternative – barging around the point into Chippewa Bay, and upward from there.

After our phone call, I turn to Margy to discuss this. Although she'd like to go with me, she dreads the thought of a trail that will require differential lockers.

"The water is pretty shallow back there," she says, rationalizing a bit on the route behind the Hole we'll need to take in the barge just to access the trail. "Lots of stumps barely underwater," she adds.

She's right, the lake level is way down, and it won't be easy to position the barge at the end of the steep trail. Now there are three strikes against the plan – no experience on this trail, it's too steep, and water that's too shallow. It adds up to a "no go" decision, but the alternative sticks in my mind.

"Would you like to go with me, if we didn't have to use that trail?" I ask.

"Sure," Margy replies. "You're thinking about the Chippewa ramp, aren't you? It would take a little longer, but maybe John would be willing to wait."

I'm back on the phone immediately.

"Hello, again," I say to John. "How about an improved plan?"

"Improved how?" he asks.

"Margy would like to see the Donkey Trail," I reply, knowing he enjoys trips when Margy can join us. "So we'll take the barge around to the Chippewa ramp, and ride up to meet you from there. It won't take much longer than riding a quad from Hole in the Wall. We could meet you by noon."

And I don't even have to use the word "chicken." There's a brief silence while John thinks this through.

"Okay," he finally replies. "But put 'er in high gear."

If there's one quality John lacks when quad riding is involved, it's patience.

* * * * *

WE DO PUT OURSELVES INTO HIGH GEAR, quickly preparing the barge for departure. The trip around to Chippewa Bay takes less than an hour, with comfortable water all the way. We find no boats at the logging dock, and no logging activity is expected today. Margy drives the barge as we approach the ramp. It's our preferred way to come ashore, since it gives me time to prepare the deck for off-load.

"Take it ashore to the left of the main ramp," I suggest before leaving the aft cab. "We can park there while we're riding today. If another barge comes in, they'll have plenty of space."

This is a luxury, since the Chippewa Dock is about a half-kilometre from the ramp, requiring extra time to walk back to our quads after docking. The only challenge will be to secure the barge to shore at the ramp, since winds on this bay can develop with no notice.

As we maneuver towards shore on the left side of the ramp, all looks good from the bow until an underwater snag appears straight ahead. I quickly evaluate the potential hazard – the bow will pass over it a few metres from shore, leaving enough clearance at the stern to be a non-factor for the prop. So I say nothing, and motion over my shoulder for Margy to continue towards shore.

I'm right about the situation – there's no hazard to the prop. But I'm wrong about the scenario, since we're in shallower water than I estimated. We come to a sudden stop on top of the submerged snag, with the center of the boat lodged on top.

"Stuck!" I yell back to Margy. "You'll have to back up to get us off."

Margy nods, and shifts into reverse. But we don't move, except to pivot a bit on top of the stump: "Gun it!" I yell back to her.

She does. And at first we don't move, and then she adds even more power, and we slowly begin to back off the snag. *Scrape. Scrape.* But this boat is tough, thick metal throughout. Slowly we slide back off into deeper water, leaving blue bottom-paint on the stump.

"Let's try again," I say to Margy when I return to the cab. "The right side this time."

So we approach the ramp again, this time on the other side where there are no stumps. The barge slides onto shore with a comfortable scrunch of metal on gravel. We off-load the quads and secure the bow with our big tie-down ropes so the barge will stay put while we're gone.

The ride up Chippewa Main to where it joins with Heather Main is always an awe-inspiring ride, with lots of sweeping view of Powell Lake below us. Margy leads, and there are places where she slows down to feel more comfortable, but we never stop until reaching our favourite overlook high above the lake. The summer air is clear and warm, and the view simply majestic.

We join Heather Main at the top, turning left towards where John will exit the Last Chance Trail. I glance at my watch: 11:45 – fifteen minutes early. What precise timing for a rough estimate. John likes it when I'm on time.

Powell Lake Overlook on Heather Main

Sure enough, after waiting only 5 minutes at the bottom of the Last Chance Trail, there's John! As I've ridden upward from Chippewa Bay, I've developed an idea I'm sure John will appreciate. He enjoys logistic challenges, and I've come up with a thought-provoking proposal to offer to him.

"Hey, John, how long would it take you to get back to your house from right here?"

I've already computed an estimate for this, since I know he'd need to ride back through the Last Chance Trail, then to his truck parked on Southview Road, and finally back along Highway 101 to town. My estimate is an hour-and-a-half.

John ponders this for only a few seconds, and replies: "Slightly over an hour."

"That's less than I thought," I admit. "Now, suppose it would take you three hours, but you could do it in a more exciting way, using four modes of transportation?"

John always likes "more exciting."

"Oh?" he replies, and I can visualize the gears in his mind turning. "Now I get it," he adds quickly. "We use the barge."

"Right!" I reply. "We ride our quads down to Chippewa and onto the barge. Then down the lake to the Shinglemill, where we get into Margy's truck and drive you back to Southview Road. Then you drive your truck to Shinglemill to pickup your quad. Three hours, but what a trip!"

Yes, it would be quite a trip. Like John, I enjoy a simple life, while using complex logistics, always an interesting challenge.

"Missing something?" says Margy.

Both John and I think about her question, and neither of us comes up with anything right away.

"Who has the keys to my truck?" she asks.

Oops. Good idea, but one element missing. All three of us have keys to Margy's truck. None of us have the keys here at the intersection with the Last Chance Trail.

"Could go back to Hole in the Wall to get the keys," suggests John.

Now that would be the epitome of the complicated simple life, best left for another day.

So we forget my grand plan, and continue with our original goal of working on the Donkey Trail. At first, the ride is easy, along a recently pruned trail that's effortless for a few klicks – flat and nearly straight. Then, suddenly, the trail gets extremely rough, over an old main that took John and his friends many hours to rejuvenate. They've laid down large sections of rocks and logs that serve as a barely adequate quad trail. John rides through it, but Margy and I park our bikes and walk the final half-klick to meet him at his quad where the recently reworked portion of the road ends.

"We've moved lots of rocks to get this far," John notes. "Not much better for the next klick, and then it gets easier for a bit."

"You've walked it all the way to the steam donkey?" I ask.

"Sure. Not a bad hike. But it'll be a bitch to re-open for a quad. Especially when it's time to drop down to the steam donkey at the end. Haven't quite figured that out yet."

But he will. He always does.

A Difficult Portion of the Donkey Trail

For the next three hours, we put old-fashioned trail building skills to use. It's basic hand labour to do what a modern road-building crew would tackle with big machines and dynamite. We're a lot smaller

John and Bro Ready to Work

scale and a whole lot slower, but we keep pressing ahead a few metres at a time.

John is in charge of blazing the direction of travel, following the old main. He cuts his way through with his chainsaw as he goes. Behind him, I'm in charge of rocks – meaning leveling the path by

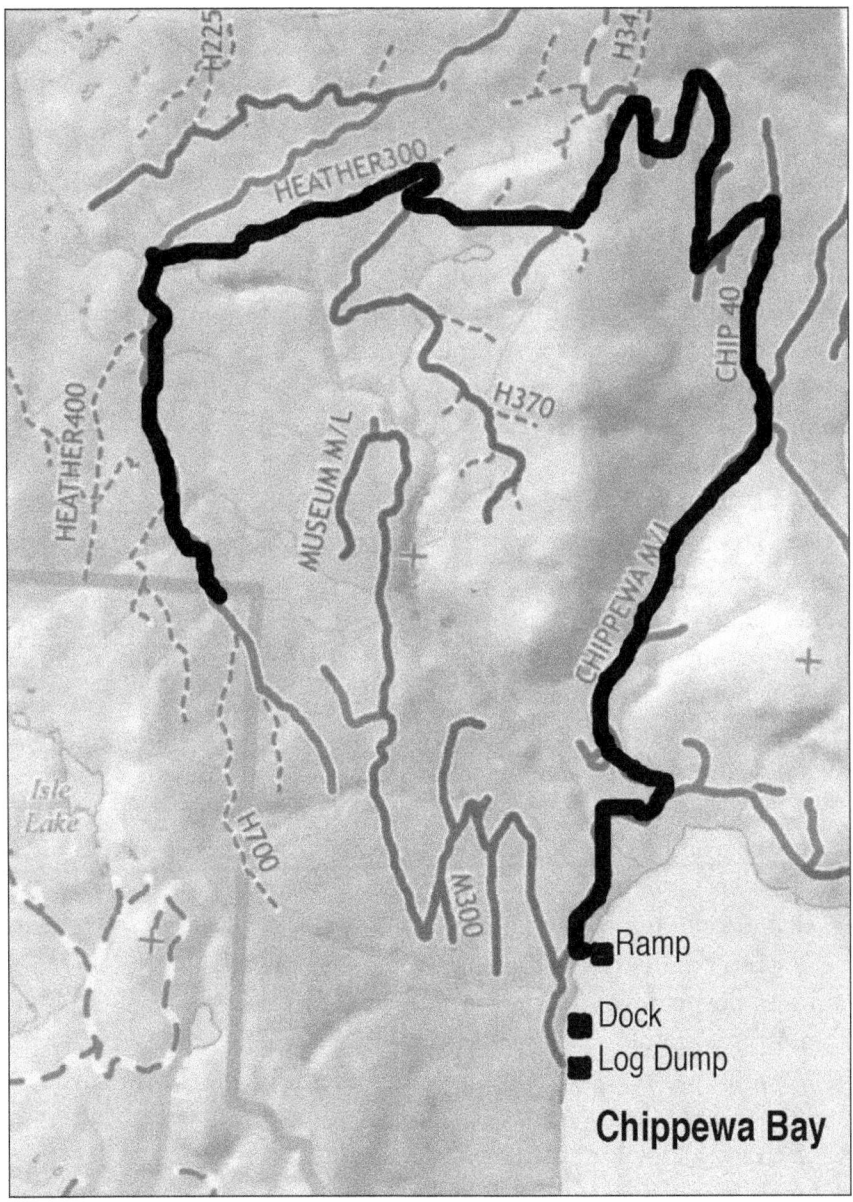

Donkey Trail Trip

moving rocks and filling in where I remove them. For this, I frequently need to call John back to my work spot, so he can help me with the bigger boulders, many of which look impossibly wedged in the packed earth. But with lots of grunts and groans, there's almost no rock we can't move.

Meanwhile, Margy works behind us. She's the "details" person, using pruning shears to cut away small branches and roots that must be removed to make the path acceptable for a quad. Together, the three of us make remarkable progress. By late afternoon, we've added nearly a half-klick to the Donkey Trail.

John has completed most of the work today, with Margy and I contributing what we can. Even when it comes to making decisions about moving rocks, I realize I'm not really qualified.

"This one is really not in the way, is it?" I say to John, referring to a boulder-size chunk that seems too imbedded to remove.

"Can't leave it there," he says. "Notice how it's in the way when you come around that corner, especially the jagged part. Could damage a quad."

John is right, of course, and he's not willing to listen to reason when it comes to immovable obstacles. So we move the big rock, mostly by digging with our hands and then wrenching with a big pry bar. Together, we finally manhandle the now-exposed boulder off to the side of the trail, John spurring me on with a round of "Push! Push!"

Finally, just when I'm convinced I don't have another ounce of energy to apply to the tasks at hand, I look back and see Margy sitting on a old stump, gulping down a bottle of water. We're both at the end of our stamina. And just in time, John declares we've gone far enough for today, as if he slyly knows and understands our situation.

"Let's stop," he says. "I'm going back to get my quad, and see what it's like to ride this new section."

I stand beside the cleared path, pressed against the bushes, as John rumbles slowly down the trail towards me. Bro is striding behind him, as fast as his chubby body can muster.

As John passes, he yells to me: "There's nothing like being first on a trail never ridden by a quad."

I think about his words for a moment. He's right – when this old main was active decades ago, there were no four-wheeled off-road recreational vehicles like ours. Times have changed, and we're here today where the previous generation could never have traveled except on foot or by logging truck. It's an old main, but a new quad trail.

It's also a reminder that a bit of physical labour and a fair amount of sweat in the rejuvenation of an old main results in a lot of personal satisfaction. A few sore muscles the next day are a small price to pay for the feeling of accomplishment when you contribute to a demanding project in the forest.

"I helped revive this old trail," I'll say to myself or someone else a few years from now. "I remember when you could hardly walk through here, before I helped move more rocks than you can imagine."

Chapter 8

Chasing the Sun
Clover Dock, Goat Island

OCTOBER BRINGS PROLONGED WARM RAIN. My rain gauge overflows well before the end of the month, which means the precipitation total exceeds 35 centimetres, a record since I've been logging rainfall totals at my cabin over the past five years. November roars in with strong winds and more rain, and we're already headed for another record month of precipitation.

When Margy and I return from the States after a week's visit, we step onto the deck of our floating cabin to discover evidence of extreme winds, including the absence of one of our prized potted trees. The missing fir was a metre-and-a-half tall, firmly rooted in a sturdy planter, and all that remains are a few of the decorative rocks that topped the soil of the pot. Hole in the Wall is a microcosm for occasional meteorological downbursts, best described as small tornadoes. We've had heavy objects lifted from the deck by the gusty winds that bounce every which way off the high cliffs during unstable atmospheric conditions. The potted tree's absence is a reminder of the severity of winds which have propelled other heavy objects off our deck, including sawhorses, chairs, propane tanks, and barbecue stoves.

After our short absence, another weather-related phenomenon is evident. The water north of First Narrows has taken on a dull green colour, extremely clouded with silt, accompanied by a plethora of small twigs and extensive floating debris. At first, I think it's the result of a nearby landslide, since there have been several on the lake during this extended period of precipitation. Or maybe these conditions are the result of heavy runoff from the many streams entering the lake at this time of year.

"It reminds me of Toba Inlet," I note to Margy. "The hue of the water in Toba looks just like this."

"But that's from glacier-fed streams," replies Margy. "Powell Lake is fed by snow and some glacier runoff in the spring, but not this time of year."

She's right. This green, silty water is new to me, and it seems to extend far to the north, at least as far as I've gone recently in my boat. In my decade-and-a-half on this lake, I've never seen conditions like this. Nor has John, which is proof we're seeing something truly unique. This autumn has already set records in both rainfall and subsequent runoff, and that seems the obvious cause. The green hue continues for several weeks, trapped here by the relatively-shallow sill in First Narrows, which separates us from the substantially deeper part of the lower lake.

When the weather momentarily clears in mid-November, I'm quick to prepare the barge for a trip to Olsen's Landing. Maybe this will be the day I break loose from this year's already-established winter blues. I'm quick to admit I'm a victim of extensive lethargy and sometimes worse when the sun doesn't shine for weeks at a time. When I lived in Southern California, it was even worse, which probably sounds backwards. But then I worked inside all day at a college campus, and when I emerged from my building in the winter months, the sun was already set. So I found myself prone to bouts of seasonal affective disorder, a near-depression that afflicted me for much of the winter. But even during the winter rains of British Columbia, I'm outside much of the day, regardless of the weather, and that seems a vast improvement from my previous imprisonment indoors. Still, winter isn't my favourite time of year. Maybe today's brief dose of sun during a barge outing will have a positive affect.

Getting the barge ready to go has become a fairly simple process, since nearly everything is already aboard. Today it's slightly more complicated. The heavy metal loading ramps have been temporarily removed and stored on the cabin deck, since they're in our way when hauling firewood. During the previous two months, Margy and I have barged to spots on the shore where driftwood has collected, loading it onto the barge for the return trip to our cabin. The empty space on the barge, even without removing our quads, is plenty big enough for our driftwood runs, as long as the big ramps are removed to allow for easier stacking of the wood.

Other than reloading the ramps, the barge is nearly ready to go. Since this will only be a day trip, it's pretty much a matter of dressing in layers to combat the cold, packing some snacks for the trip, and starting the outboard motor. All aboard – off we go.

We head north towards our intended destination, Olsen's Landing. As we pass Elvis Point, I motor in close to get a look at the new floating cabin of unusual design – two residences on the same float, with a connecting roof between them. "Graceland," as it's called, has recently been towed from the Shinglemill, where it was built. It's a beautiful structure – a mansion in terms of float cabins – fit for a king (Elvis, that is). Next to the floating edifice, on the upper part of the headlands, is a life-size wooden statue of Elvis Presley, crooning into his microphone. How this all began is anyone's guess, but Elvis Point has been a landmark for as long as anyone seems to remember. Personally, I liked the previous statue of Elvis with his big guitar, but student pranksters carried that wooden shrine away a decade ago.

"The water is just as green here as it is at our cabin," says Margy, noting the continuing silty trend.

"Imagine how much runoff it would take to maintain this weirdness," I reply.

Maybe it's my somewhat sour mood from the prolonged lack of sunlight, but I linger on thoughts of these green silty conditions for a few minutes. Of course, you can't help but wonder if global warming is somehow to blame. Also, what about all of the other headline items that question the changes in our environment? The first thing that comes to mind is the recent news story involving the accelerating decline in the global animal population – the ongoing Holocene Extinction Event, seemingly related to human activity. Yet this important headline came and went in 2014 with little fanfare. And what about the recent demise of starfish along the BC coast? Sea-stars are losing their legs along enormous expanses of shoreline, a baffling wasting disease that dissolves their bodies into goo. One thing reminds me of another – substantial groves of arbutus trees have died out along the shores of Powell Lake this year. When I'm gloomy because of the weather (and the bigger scope of climate change), it can extend to nearly unlimited fits of despondency.

Margy obviously can't read my mind, but suddenly she shakes me out of my dreary mood by interrupting my train of thought.

"You know, we should take a look at Clover Dock when we pass by," she suggests. "If there aren't any boats, why not go there instead of Olsen's?"

"Why not?" I respond. "Even though it's a weekday, if there aren't any boats, there's no logging or road-building going on."

We originally picked Olsen's Landing as our destination because it's relatively close to our cabin and inactive in terms of logging these days. But Clover Main Dock on Goat Island is even closer, and we'll be passing right by it on our way to Olsen's. As is typical of us, Margy and I are quick to change our destination at the drop of a hat. In fact, it's one of the things that makes voyaging together so much fun. We never know where we'll end up until we get there. For two people known to friends as being extremely organized and intent on their goals, we tend to give in to whims of the moment when we travel. Which is a happy thing. And so it is today.

Approaching the promontory before Clover Dock, I delay longer than normal in my preparation of the barge deck for our arrival. I'm not certain this dock nor Olsen's Landing will be empty of work boats today, and we won't be going ashore at either location if there's evidence of logging or road-building. Considering the shortness of daylight hours, we'll simply turn around and head home, nevertheless enjoying our brief excursion. Since we might not be unloading our quads, I've decided to leave preparation procedures for offloading until we're sure we're going ashore.

"Looks empty," says Margy, as soon as Clover Dock is in sight.

"Okay, I'll need some extra time to get the quads ready," I reply. "Why don't you drive for a while? Maybe we should hover off-shore over there."

Margy takes control of the helm, and begins to maneuver the barge towards a loitering point about a half-kilometre from the dock. Meanwhile, I go out onto the deck, and begin to remove the covers from our quads. Normally, our bikes ride on the barge naked most of the summer, always ready to go. But the rainy months have moved in, so we keep them covered, and it takes a few extra minutes to take care of the tarps. Then I proceed through the normal process – unchain the bikes, fuel valves on, wheel chocks removed, cargo straps untied. Finally, I start up the quad engines to let them warm up for a quick off-load. We've learned that actions should be minimal once we ground ourselves to shore, in case the barge starts to drift.

By now, we have the process down to a science. With minimal need to communicate, we start through our self-assigned duties. Margy maneuvers us towards the barge ramp, while I go to the bow to watch for underwater obstacles and to prepare to disembark as soon as we hit ground. Margy sets up a nice drift towards shore, switches the outboard into neutral and tilts the engine partially up to clear potential submerged obstacles. We touch land at a nearly perfect right angle, with negligible forward speed – a flawless arrival. I'm off the bow in a flash, and begin to pull the metal ramps into position. In

Author at Clover Barge Ramp

just a few minutes, we're off-loaded, and I give the boat a push back into deeper water while Margy shifts into reverse. Then she backs us expertly towards the dock, where we'll leave the barge while we're riding.

When we get back to our parked quads, Margy tries to get a photo of the scene. Even though it's still early in the day, shadows have already engulfed the area near the barge ramp, so her camera automatically activates its flash mode – near high-noon.

I've come here hoping to find the sun, as a proposed cure for my cloudy-skies funk. So in the instant of this photograph at the barge ramp, I think about how badly I need solar rays. Or, perhaps more realistically, I "think" that lack of sunlight is on the top of my agenda.

In a few more minutes, we're on the road, headed towards an extension of Clover Main we've not previously explored. On our last trip along this road, we ventured a considerable distance to the northeast, but stopped when we ran out of time. Today we'd like to go as far as the road allows, although I'm not sure how far that will be. I know this main gets more overgrown as you pass the turnoff to Frogpond, but we'll see how much farther we can go.

We climb up and away from the barge ramp area, entering an intense blast of cold-soaked sun in the staging area above the dock. Yes! – sunlight! It feels good.

From here, we drive in and out of the shadow of Goat Island's midday light, progressing into and out of shade as trees along the road set the scene. Soon after passing Clover Main's 3-kilometre red-and-white marker sign, a well-groomed trail peels off to our left. Margy, who is in the lead, pulls over to the side of the road and stops. She's obviously interested in seeing where this trail will lead, since it seems angled towards Clover Lake.

When we get off our bikes to inspect the trail further, it appears muddy and challenging, maybe best tackled on-foot. So we begin to hike down toward Clover Lake.

The trail is short and not so saturated that we can't step over the puddles. It ends at the log-choked south shore, where a makeshift dock has been constructed. A raft with a small outboard motor is tied up here, and another small fibreglass boat is overturned on shore nearby. During summer, this is an obvious lazy oasis for those who know about the trail. Except for today's 3-degree temperature and the absence of leaves from the few deciduous trees mixed in with the evergreens, it looks a lot like summer.

Back on the main, we travel north past the Frogpond turnoff, and uphill on the deteriorating main that becomes increasingly overgrown from both sides and in the center hump. Margy leads, shifting from one side of the road to the other as conditions change. Finally, she decides it's not worth struggling any farther, so we turn around to explore some of the spurs off the main we've passed along the way. They are all short, ending in impassable dead ends. But it's fun trying to get through, and we've been in and out of the sun the entire journey, so I'm smiling inside my helmet.

We return towards the logging dock, traveling through the truck staging area to seek Elvis Main. This is an old logging road I traveled with John many years ago on our 100 cc motorbikes. Even then, the old main was approaching overgrown, and now it's even worse. But

Clover Lake

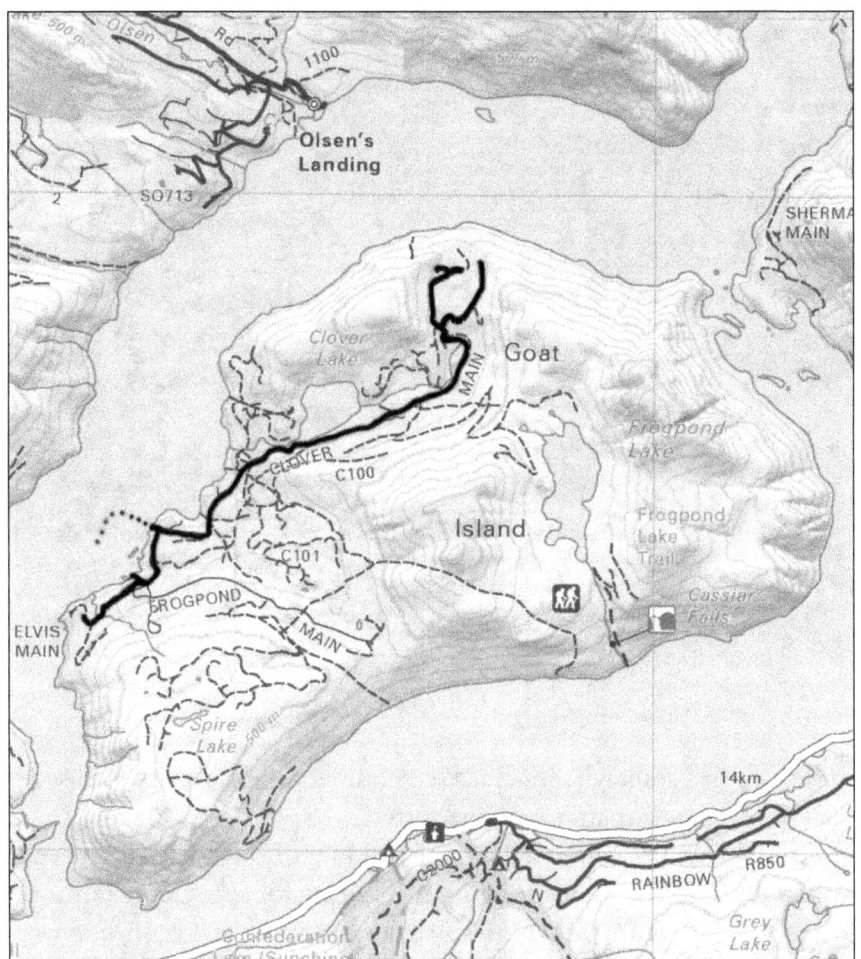

Clover Dock Trip

we press on, driving through difficult conditions to see how far we can go.

Judging by the lack of tire treads and the preponderance of overhanging branches, no one has been through here in quite awhile. I stop occasionally at some particularly rough spots to use my pruning shears to cut our way through. Still, we keep going until we reach the Y-junction that splits Elvis Main. According to my map, we're less than a kilometre from Elvis Point, but the road conditions are now awful,

Elvis Main

so we stop in a somewhat uncluttered chunk of the old main to absorb the last remnants of afternoon warmth.

The November sun may be brief and low to the horizon, but you can find it in spots. After sitting in the clearing for a few more minutes to recharge my human batteries, we turn around and push our way through the branches and small trees, back to the logging dock.

It's become a continuing battle for glimpses of sun lately. And so for another four months, I'll chase the elusive sunlight into winter, enjoying its rejuvenating power whenever I can.

* * * * *

THE FOLLOWING AUTUMN, another chasing-the-sun trip begins under different circumstances. This time, in early October, a sunny period is ending, and it's time to take advantage of the weather before it disappears. The morning dawns bright, with a solar halo as an indicator of upper-level ice particles marking the approach of a coastal storm. Since we've become accustomed to leaving our quads in the ready-to-go mode, even with shortened daylight hours it's easy to make a midday departure and be home before dark.

There's a short ride Margy has been thinking about since the past summer, when a friend from California came to visit. He and I rode into the old village near Olsen's Creek that was eventually abandoned and later purposely set afire by the RCMP. From that summer ride, I brought home photos of an elaborate old cellar and tales of artifacts. No one appreciates relics of old residences in the forest more than Margy.

So we set off for Olsen's Landing under mackerel skies "more wet than dry." It's a short trip up the lake, and as we approach shore at Olsen's, all my preparations out on the deck are quickly complete. I move to the bow and stand there, waiting for Margy to put us ashore without the need for any shouted instructions or even hand signals. She drives the route to shore so well that it's simply a gentle *bump-bump*, and we're against the gravel beach.

Our off-load is quick, and we're on our way up Olsen's Main. It's a short trip to the turnoff to the left. As anticipated, the entrance to the trail to Olsen's Creek and the village is beyond Margy's comfort zone. We've both expected this, so I simply switch into four-wheel drive and push forward, jostling through the deep trench and up the other side. Then I walk back to retrieve Margy's quad to ride it through, while she hikes through.

Once we're back on our quads on the other side of the deep cut, it's an easy ride the rest of the way. I go first, leading Margy past the initial traces of the old homestead, where I know she wants to stop. First, we'll ride to the creek for a lunch snack. At this majestic spot overlooking the creek, we are amazed by a major washout that has left huge trees toppled along a severely eroded bank.

Looking out over this devastated area, it's easy to imagine the intensity of the water as it flooded through here the previous year. And we remember the extensive period of cloudy, green water in Powell Lake. We surmise that the unusual accumulation of silty water began here. Of course, there's nothing to prove this was the place where that major washout began, but just looking at the demolished bend in the creek is enough evidence to convince us. Besides, the outlet of Olsen's

Creek, only a few kilometres downstream, is now a jumble of rocks and logs, more confirmation that this was the source of the extensive green silty water that extended all the way down the lake.

After our brief stop at the creek, we return along the trail to the old homestead, where previous visitors have arranged artifacts against the trees and around the exposed foundation – kitchen pans, cups, utensils, car parts, an extensive exhibit of plumbing relics, and even a bathtub posed as if it has just been used. To us, the highlight is the deep cellar that marks the history of a large home (as documented in historic reports, although it looks to me like a community building). Cement sidewalks, still in relatively good condition, fan out to flattened outbuildings and debris sites.

Margy is thrilled by what we see, and I remain in awe from my previous visit. We stroll around, pleased to find artifacts that represent the respect past travelers have exercised during their visits to this site. Leaving these antique remnants for all to enjoy is a sign of caring remembrance.

Old Homestead

It's a warm day for October, but the sun is mostly behind the clouds now, a precursor to the storm scheduled to move in tonight. As we explore, I enjoy the muted sunlight, and then it's time to leave. We ride back out to the trail's entrance, where I ferry our two quads through the deep trench and out onto Olsen's Main. From here we ride leisurely up to Olsen's Lake, where we pause for a few minutes, looking over the water towards the tall peaks to the east. Even under increasingly cloudy skies, this is one of the most awe-inspiring locations in the region. We've chased the sun again in autumn, and found it lingering quietly in the wilderness.

Olsen's Lake

Center-of-Book Photos

Behind John's Cabin Number 2, Hole in the Wall, Powell Lake BC

No Name Barge Ramp, Goat Lake BC

Chippewa Bay South Logging Area

John and Bro at Chip South

John, Mike, and Margy at Kinsman's Beach (Shinglemill)

Author with John and Bro at Kinsman's Beach

Steam Donkey on Museum Main, Chippewa Bay

Chapter 9

2-Trees
Spire Main, Goat Island

With overnight camping trips now out of the question for at least five months, November moves into its first below-zero evenings. Trips on the barge have reverted to day excursions, and the sun-filled hours are limited. At our cabin, because of the constraints of the cliffs and nearby trees, sunrise is after 9 o'clock, and the sun dips behind the trees to the southwest shortly after noon. Thus, there are only three hours of direct sunshine, followed by another four hours of shadowed, subdued light until a concealed sunset behind the Bunster Range to the west. Days are short, and they will get shorter still for another full month. For all practical aspects, this is already the winter solstice.

Quad trips in the barge are shorter now, but that's fine with Margy and me. We enjoy brief cold-weather rides, and we seek locations where most of the riding can be accomplished in direct sunlight. This eliminates destinations on the west shore of the lake, blocked from the sun in the early afternoon by the Bunsters and western ridges farther north.

Dunn Dock, on the south side of Goat Island, is a notable exception. It receives afternoon sun from the southwest, so it's an obvious destination for a late November day. Plus, I'm still intent on finding "2-Trees," the huge old-growth firs I view from my cabin on the high ridge of Goat Island (Chapter 5). I keep thinking about how close I must have been to these giant trees when we climbed high above the Dunn Main dock on BC Day weekend.

Today I've brought my chainsaw with me, strapped to the front rack of my quad – ready to cut through the blocked spur that may have kept me from my goal that summer day.

All goes well at Goat Island's Dunn Dock, and we're off-loaded from the barge and on our way efficiently. But in only a klick, it becomes obvious that one of the recent storms has taken its toll on the lower portion of Dunn Main. Even before we reach the turnoff to Spire Main, we run into two obstacles. I'm able to remove the first line of fallen branches by hand, but then we come to a big log that's fallen across the road, less than 2 kilometres from the dock. When I survey the half-metre trunk, I realize it will be a lengthy process to cut our way through. The log lies flat on the ground, so it will require two complete cuts, and I'm not sure my saw is up to the task. John would tackle this job, and somehow defeat it quickly, but it might take me an hour. And with two obstacles in such a short distance, who's to say there isn't another a short distance beyond. This could be an all-afternoon process, and afternoons are short this time of year.

I get off my bike, and survey the possibilities. Margy says nothing, but I know what she's thinking.

"Kinda hopeless, don't you think?" I suggest.

"Not worth it," she concurs.

"Good excuse for a barge ride though," I add.

She laughs, and agrees: "We said this would have to be a short ride, but even shorter than I expected. Enough for me though."

"Me, too."

We're easily satisfied, and pleased to experience a boat ride in the November sun. So we turn our quads around, and head back down to the dock. There will be other days.

* * * * *

THERE'S ANOTHER WAY TO GET TO SPIRE MAIN. With the possibility that lower Dunn Main will remain closed for the remainder of the winter because of the fallen log, it makes sense to consider accessing Spire Main from Clover Dock to the north. We can climb quickly to the junction with Spire Main, and then back to the routes that seem most promising to reach 2-Trees. The spur with the fallen log on BC Day and also the area where we walked beyond considerable fallen timber are two possible paths to the big trees. From a combination of logging company maps and the track provided by my GPS during our summer trip, I know we were close to 2-Trees.

So we plan to travel back to Clover Dock, and then ride south and upward to Spire Main. But when prolonged winter weather systems and our intervening personal schedules conspire to keep us grounded, it isn't until April that we're able to make the trip. And when we do, it won't be along the route we'd expected from Clover Dock. Sometimes when you're hunting ghost trees, it leads to phantom trails.

* * * * *

LOGGING ACTIVITY MOVES AROUND rapidly on the lake. Chippewa South, where we rode along a newly constructed main less than a year ago, is now abandoned, after a seemingly short period of falling activity. And for now, Goat Island's Clover Dock is the focus of extensive road-building and tree harvesting, so we've missed our opportunity to tackle Spire Main by the back door. Meanwhile, activity on the south side of the island at Dunn Main seems much more tranquil. The fallen log that stopped my climb from Dunn Dock in November may still stretch across the road, or maybe someone has removed it. My saw has a new chain, and I feel more prepared to tackle this big log, if necessary. From this southerly approach to Spire Main, I'll be headed directly into the high country to make another attempt at finding 2-Trees.

So on a beautiful April day, Margy and I depart with our route seemingly decided. First we'll travel the short distance to Chip South, to ride this now abandoned logging area. It should be fun comparing what we find today to the completely different environment less than a year ago when we rode the just-constructed main. The views overlooking the lake should be spectacular, since the trees beside the road are now gone. Chip South's short roads (one north, one south) should take only an hour, so we plan to travel from there to Dunn Dock.

As on most days, the calm conditions in Hole in the Wall mean little about the conditions on the rest of the lake. I'm lured into a sense of complacency as we start south through the tranquil conditions in First Narrows. Since this is such a short trip in the barge, I decide to get going with my preparation for landing while Margy drives out into the North Sea. It will be nice to relax as we approach Chip South, not needing to climb out on the deck to do the chores I normally save until closer to our destination. After all, the voyage will be short, and the lake is calm.

No sooner do I unstrap the quads than we hit whitecaps. By now, besides the straps, I've disconnected the safety chain connecting the two quads to the side rail. Our bikes begin to bob up and down on their shocks as we plow through the waves. It's a short distance through the edge of the North Sea, and then across the mouth of Chippewa Bay to the dock at Chip South, but I should have known better. John's nickname of "North Sea" wasn't without forethought. And Chippewa Bay is famous for winds known as CB CBer's, another moniker invented by John -- Chippewa Bay Cabin Busters.

Margy is quick to react to the conditions, which she finds uncomfortable. She undoubtedly wonders why I untied the quads so early, even for such a short voyage, and she doesn't like what she sees.

"Oh! Oh!" she yells when I return from the barge deck. "I don't like this! Our bikes are jumping all over the place."

"Stop here, and I'll go out and strap them back down," I offer in an obviously disgusted tone.

I'm mad at myself, not her. And Margy is trying to act brave by slowing the boat, but not stopping.

"Aren't you nervous?" she asks.

"Park is park," I reply confidently, although not sure she understands I'm talking about the gear the quads are in. "Park is even better than a parking brake, as far as I'm concerned."

"They look like they're ready to jump overboard!"

She's right (mostly). So am I (less so). Our quads look precarious, and I'm tempted to tell her to stop the boat, so I can go out onto the deck and tie them down again. But Margy presses on without stopping, obviously still nervous about the situation. The barge's reduced speed doesn't seem to help the bouncing.

"I promise not to untie the quads so early next time," I relent.

It's too little, too late, but I feel better for saying it.

Fortunately, the path across the rough water is short, and we're soon lined up for approach to the Chip South barge ramp, with a wind that will push us directly towards shore, which is as good as it gets (other than no wind at all). Margy drives us straight into the ramp, and makes firm, safe contact with the shore. The barge stays straight and steady in the wind.

I pull the metal off-load ramps into position, a process that steadies us even more. There will be no problem with the quads now, but the weather conditions aren't favorable for leaving our barge against the shore while we're riding.

"We'll need to move over to the dock after we off-load," I say. "Too bad – we'll only be gone a short while."

"And we'll have to move it back, for the on-load," adds Margy. "Who knows what will happen to the wind in the meantime."

Two minds already thinking alike. It happens to us a lot.

"Want to skip it?" I ask. "We can head to Dunn Main right now. With south winds, Dunn should be a lot more protected."

"Let's go," she replies.

It's as simple as that. Margy goes back to the cab, while I pull the metal ramps back aboard. I push off shore, accompanied by her backing the barge out against the wind. Margy tracks straight rearward, swings the barge around, and we're on our way to a new destination. Two like minds thinking alike is a joy when decisions can be made so quickly.

Headed back across the North Sea, conditions improve. Rather than being thrust into the whitecaps, we're now pushed by trailing seas. I've secured our quad straps again, which makes us both feel more comfortable, and this time I'll leave them on until we're closer to our destination.

Passing Cassiar Island, we follow the south side of the lake to see if Doug is at his cabin today. When we pass Pickle Point, wave conditions improve even more, falling in the wind-shadow of the shore, and it looks almost calm ahead.

Doug's new dock looks finished, but there's no boat his cabin, so Margy aims us across the water to the headland where Dunn Dock sits protected from the now nearly nonexistent winds. This is a Saturday, and there are no boats at the dock, so we feel assured we won't run into road-builders or loggers today.

Margy's approach to the barge ramp is perfect. This has been her day at the helm, and I never touch the wheel during the entire day. She loves this boat as much as I do, and handles it superbly.

We off-load and tie up the barge to big boulders. If no one is here now, no logging crews will be coming this late in the day. We leave enough room to the side in case a recreational landing craft wants to come ashore, and off we go on our quads.

Fresh equipment tracks on the road make me confident the log obstacle we encountered in November is gone, but I watch my old GPS track as we proceed. Soon we're at the GPS location of the old log, and the main is clear. The road remains in excellent shape all the way up.

When we finally reach the high road that cuts across the island to Clover Dock, we suddenly see towering equipment ahead. Our progress comes to a grinding stop. Three center-of-the-road machines, a marvel of modern forestry engineering, seem to block our path completely.

At first, I think this is the end of our trip today, but Margy walks ahead and reports: "I think we can get through. It looks like they left a path just wide enough for a quad."

Maybe it's a coincidence, but there's a winding course we can follow to get around the big equipment. So we follow it, and are

Margy at Logging Equipment Blocking the Road

quickly past the obstacles. From here, the road is wide and recently rejuvenated. Obviously, this equipment has come in from the other side of the island at Clover Dock.

I lead the way now, turning off at Spire Main, where we climb towards the prospective location of 2-Trees. When we arrive at the turnoff where we previously had to turn around, I confront the same tree that blocked our path nearly a full year ago on my first quest for 2-Trees.

My saw with its new chain makes quick work of the small log. As expected, there are further obstacles ahead, but I'm able to cut through these obstructions as well. I stop at each, start my saw, and re-open another section of the trail with one or two cuts. This goes on for about 2 kilometres, requiring a half-dozen stops to get to the end of the road.

New fallen logs are plentiful and huge here, but now it's obvious this isn't really the end of the old road, but merely a spot where it splits into a "Y," with two overgrown, rough paths leading farther.

"Let's see how far we can walk," I say to Margy.

"You go ahead, and I'll keep me own pace behind you."

This is a good plan, since the obstacles require a lot of log-hopping, which isn't an area of expertise for Margy. So I plod ahead, following the first leg of the "Y," hopefully towards 2-Trees.

This spur ends abruptly, and it's thick forest ahead, impenetrable without a lot of slogging through rough terrain. Yet I feel I'm near the ridge overlooking Hole in the Wall, although I can't see the water. In the bright sunlight reflecting off my GPS, it's difficult to tell exactly where I am, but I'll sort it out afterwards back at the cabin, using my track to verify our travels today. My gut feeling, however, is that I need to go farther north to find 2-Trees.

So I backtrack to the "Y" intersection, meeting Margy along the way, and we try the other spur that's in even worse condition than the first. We catch a glimpse of Powell Lake along the way, and I still think we're too far south. Margy, on the other hand, feels we're north of the Hole. (Go ahead and guess who's right.)

All around us are big trees, similar to the tall ridge-topping giants I'm pursuing. But nowhere do two big trees stand alone in the silhouette I'm looking for. I scan side-to-side in front of me, looking for the obvious signature of these ridge-topping trees, and they're nowhere to be seen.

Once again, this second spur terminates in an end-of-road jumble of rocks and logs. Like the first road, this one finishes with a view of dense forest and a rough path that, at first, looks like an old trail. Then I realize it's a small creek bed at its upper origins, headed down to Powell Lake.

I try walking the creek for a short distance, but it becomes tough to follow, dry at this time of the year. Probably in wetter years, this creek would be roaring in April. In any case, the path is difficult, it's getting late in the day, and I must turn around without finding 2-Trees, if they're even nearby.

I'm defeated today in my quest, although I've explored some beautiful territory with lots of tall, old trees. If, as I think, we're still south of our objective, there's no other conceivable road leading to the ridge where these big trees reside. Yet loggers obviously left these two old-growth giants in a slash. And a slash means a road for access, however old it might be. Still, I feel defeated, with no prospective direction to go from here. So with a sense of end-of-the-story, we descend back down to Dunn Dock, and then home to Hole in the Wall.

Later that night, I get my first detailed look at today's GPS track. Comparing it to the logging map, I'm surprised to discover that my judgment of being south of Hole in the Wall at the Y-intersection was wrong. Just as Margy suspected, we were to the north. This means there's another possible route to 2-Trees, farther up Spire Main, just past Spire Lake. There's still hope, and another excuse for returning to the beauty of the high ridges of Goat Island.

* * * * *

MY NEXT VISIT TO SPIRE MAIN is in early May when I arrange to meet Dave and Marg at Mowat Bay on a warm and sunny Saturday. Margy and I have prepared the barge in advance by moving our two 450 cc Kodiaks sideways and as far aft as possible. By jostling the bikes around (surprisingly easy), we've turned them 90 degrees to allow plenty of room for loading a big Grizzly on the bow. Today, Dave and Margy will double on their quad, and we'll head for Dunn Dock on

2-Trees as seern from Hole in the Wall

Goat Island, a place I'm becoming intimately familiar with during my quest for 2-Trees.

Dave is the perfect riding companion for this trip. He's one of the most knowledgeable riders in the region, and he knows the local geography of forestry areas in extreme detail. Since he's seldom been on Goat Island, it's amazing how prepared he is for this trip. Yesterday, he phoned Stewart to discuss Western Forest Products' weekend plans for Goat Island. Although Stewart always answers my inquiries, it's usually delayed a bit by the phone tag necessary for a busy forestry manager. Yet Dave's contact is almost immediate, probably because he knows Stewart's private line from serving together on a variety of forestry committees. Dave is quick to bring me up to date on what to expect on Goat Island.

"Stewart said they may be hauling today, but it'll be exclusively down the other side of the island to the dock on the northwest side," says Dave, referring to what I call Clover Dock. "It's about fifty-fifty whether their harvesting equipment will be in our way. When they park it for the weekend, they're not under any obligation to leave the roads unblocked."

I know I was lucky to find the route from Dunn to Spire Main navigable (barely) on a quad several weeks ago when I encountered the three giant logging machines on the upper plateau. Maybe we'll be similarly lucky today. In any case, Dave and Marg are as flexible as Margy and me when it comes to where we end up on a trip. As I suggest to Dave: "Why don't we just see what happens, and if the road is blocked, we'll go somewhere else."

"Sounds good to me," agrees Dave.

Loading their big Grizz at Mowat Bay is a simple process. I'm able to tie up to the dock close enough to shore to allow the barge's big metal ramps to extend across a metre of water to the concrete dry portion of the launch ramp. In just a few minutes, Dave has the Grizzly up and in-place.

During the trip up the lake, Margy drives the barge, while Marg rides with her in the cab. (You'd think that a "Margy" and a "Marg" on a day-long trip would be a bit confusing, but it never is, even through I routinely call Margy "Marg" when we're alone. "Hey, Marg. Where's Marg's helmet?")

Meanwhile, Dave and I relax on the deck, sitting on two adjacent quads, enjoying the beautiful weather. I pick Dave's brain whenever we're together, trying to absorb some of his boundless knowledge regarding local forestry. Today, he explains how Western Forest Products, which has the logging contracts for almost all of the Powell Lake area, self-polices requirements regarding the panoramic spread of their clear-cut areas.

"There are at least seven official viewpoints on Powell Lake where they check the visual spread of logging areas. The limit is ten percent on the panoramic scale of viewing. That explains why that new area at Chip South is so narrow," he says, pointing to the freshly logged area a few kilometres in front of us. "Once it greens up after ten or fifteen years, they can go in again and log some more."

"Besides what you see, there are places where the harvesting methods are completely different," he explains. "For example, there's a lot of 'single-tree removal' going on by helicopter. If the trees are good

3 Quads on Barge at Mowat Bay

enough, that can be economical for a logging company. So they take a tree here and there by helicopter, and that doesn't even show up as a blip on the visual panorama."

Halfway through our trip up the lake, I exchange places with Margy. I drive the barge east from Cassiar Island, angling across towards Dunn Dock, setting up for an easy approach in today's nearly calm conditions.

With the four of us working together, we have the three quads ashore in just a few minutes. Then I take the barge over to the dock to tie-up while we explore Goat Island.

Margy leads, and I follow close behind, sometimes pulling abreast to give her the feeling of downhill protection during precipitous spots in the climb. Dave and Marg follow behind me, all of us with lights on in case we encounter any logging vehicles. There'll probably be no recreational riders on this side of the island today, judging from the empty dock, but there could be logging vehicles coming up from the other side.

We're barely underway, just approaching the center-of-island plateau, when I realize the four-wheel drive symbol is still illuminated on my instrument display. I remember dropping down off the barge in four-wheel mode, and de-selecting it immediately after that, so now I slow almost to a halt and try the switch again. Sometimes a quick toggle of the four-wheel drive switch works, but it often takes a short distance before the dashboard symbol is extinguished. And often you can't change modes until completely stopped. It's an inexact science that quad riders are used to, so I decide to come to a complete stop this time, and try again. But when I do, my bike seems to be running particularly rough.

Meanwhile, Margy has rounded the hairpin curve in front of me, making the final climb to the flat region above. In my rearview mirror, I see Dave and Marg quickly approaching from behind. I'd like to solve this problem before they arrive. Dave has a knack for finding humour in my riding abilities, which I simultaneously appreciate and abhor. I've justifiably earned a lot of friendly criticism from more experienced riders, and Dave sees right through me. For example, he knows I get lost a lot on quad trails Never, of course, really lost – just temporarily unsure of my position. And my equipment knowledge is far inferior to his, which often shows.

But when I switch into neutral and try to rev up the engine, still trying to extinguish the four-wheel light, the motor bogs down and quits. I try a quick restart, watching the quad lights in my mirror, almost on top of me now. *Grind, grind, grind* – no start.

Just as Dave pulls abeam, I look down at my handlebars and see the problem. My choke is half open, left that way after I started the quad on the barge in preparation for off-load. As we've climbed higher, the mixture has become richer, and now it won't support combustion at this altitude.

"Problems?" says Dave, ready to hop off his bike and assist.

"Just figured it out," I reply, pointing to the choke knob.

I push the choke to the off position with a bit of flare. Then I push the starter, and the engine comes to life instantaneously.

"I was running at half-choke," I say. "Running too rich."

Dave smiles, and scrunches his face into a half-questioning mode that tells me he caught me again.

"Oh, yeah," he kids.

So we're off again, with my four-wheel light now gone. We catch Margy at the top of the hill.

"I saw you stop," she explains. "But I didn't want to interrupt my climb, so I just came up here to wait for you."

"No problem," I reply. "It was just me, leaving my choke half-on until I stalled at the higher altitude."

I see her look down at her own handlebars, and then I watch her move her choke into the full-off position.

"Guess who drove your quad off the barge that way?" I admit.

She laughs, and now everyone has been treated to a version of my slip-shod bike operations. But it's all in fun, and today will be a wonderful sun-filled trip by quad and barge for all four of us. We'll be fully worn out by the end of the day, but in a most wonderful way.

* * * * *

WE PASS THE SPOT where Margy and I found the three big logging machines last month, without anything blocking the road. The slash has expanded, and more logging is evident, but we're able to proceed to Spire Main, and then up to where I turned off on the spur that we thought would take us to 2-Trees. That trail led us too far north, so now I know the road to Spire Lake is more in line with the big trees. So we continue up the main

I stop occasionally to discuss my target with Dave. I've explained to him that I never saw Spire Lake on my earlier trips, so maybe I stopped too soon when confronted with fallen trees blocking the old road on my first trip. Or maybe I drove right past Spire Lake and never saw it among the trees. Or (another maybe) if I had hiked farther, I would have been able to look down towards Hole in the Wall and might have found 2-Trees.

A little farther up Spire Main, Dave honks his horn, and I stop for him to catch up. When he pulls up beside me, he points out the lake now slightly behind us to the left, half-hidden in the trees, and asks: "Do you want me to leave some trail marking tape to identify it for you?"

I'm not sure whether this is his way of kidding me about missing the lake on my first trip. Probably, so I laugh, and then I know he's kidding when he laughs in return. Always lost!

We're finally stopped by the same logs across the road that stopped us last year, and Dave is quick to park and grab his chainsaw.

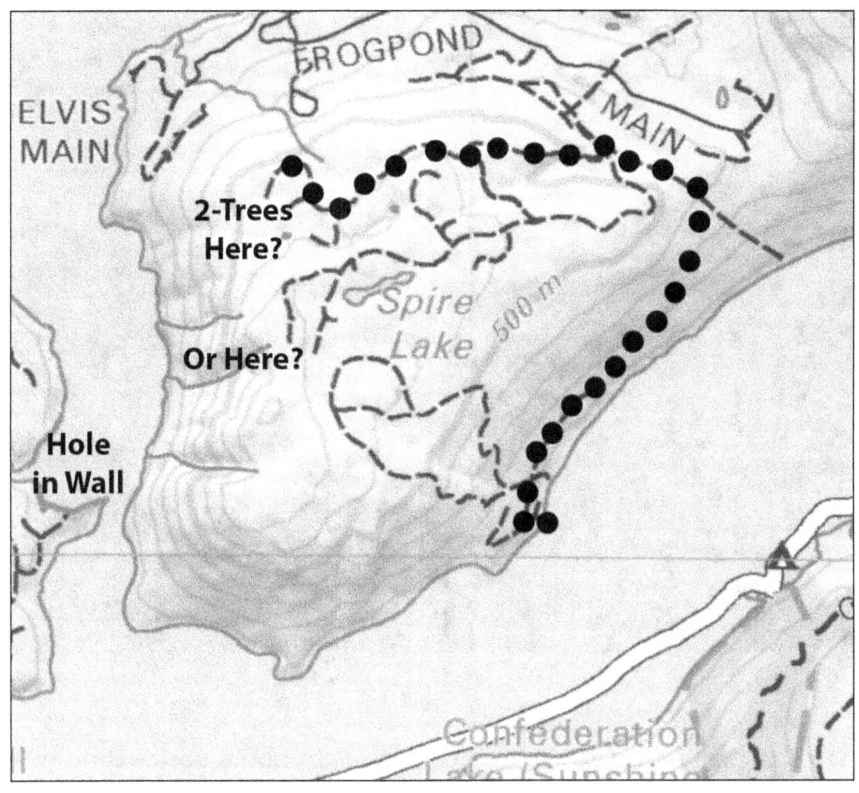

Looking for 2-Trees

"Might go on forever," I suggest. "I can see at least three more fallen trees blocking the road up ahead."

I've learned you can be easily deceived, and cutting logs that unblock a trail may lead to an almost endless string of more logs ahead. It can quickly become a losing cause.

"I'll walk ahead and check it out," I say.

"And I'll get start cutting, until I hear you yell back what you find."

So I hike ahead, over the two additional visible logs, find still another, and then it's good going for as far as I can see forward.

"Looks pretty good ahead!" I yell.

"Okay!" I hear Dave reply.

By the time I get back to Dave, he's already cut the first two logs, so I start to unstrap my chainsaw to assist. But before I even lift the

Spire Lake

saw out of my quad's forward box, Dave is finishing up the third tree. This guy is fast!

Dave has cut an opening wide enough for our quads, with only a few inches extra. He has an uncanny ability to judge exact dimensions, so his saw cuts the exact amount needed, no more and no less.

We drive ahead now, stopping at a few more places to cut our way through, but the road is surprisingly good. Then we reach an intersection, where we can take the low road (that looks totally unobstructed) or the higher road that's immediately blocked by at least two fallen trees.

"How about trying the clear road first," I say, pointing to the low road.

"I think the big trees you're looking for are on the upper trail, but we might as well check out the open road first," says Dave.

Why he thinks the upper route is the right one isn't clear to me. I've told him only a little about what I've learned so far by my combination of previous rides and GPS map triangulation of sight lines from Hole in the Wall. But if he thinks it's the upper road, I bet he's right.

Still, I want to see what's on the lower route, so I lead the way. Margy follows, and then Dave and Marg. I ride about a kilometre until the old main ends in a slash. Looking around me, there are several trees that look just like what I'm looking for, except they are solitary giant old growth trees rather than a pair. Plus, we still can't look down on Hole in the Wall or anywhere on Powell Lake. My big trees and the Hole are still quite a ways uphill on the ridge. To climb through this old, rough slash seems almost beyond comprehension, at least today.

When I turn around at the end of the lower road, the other two quads meet me, and we stop for a rest break. Bugs are swarming a bit now, but we take some time to enjoy our lunch snacks, and discuss the 2-Trees mystery some more.

"Look here on my GPS," I say to Dave. "I put a waypoint marker where I think the trees are located, and we're parked just below them, according to the map."

"And the upper road should curve this way, too," he replies. "And that's where your trees will be."

It feels exceedingly good to realize Dave's judgment regarding the most probable location of the trees matches mine. On my GPS, we're situated only 300 metres from 2-Trees. Of course, my mark on the map is only an estimate, but it's certainly encouraging. Then again, the uphill slog through the old slash is daunting.

After our lunch break, we ride back to the intersection and start uphill towards the fallen trunks that block the road. Once again, before I can get my saw out of its compartment, Dave has already finished cutting. There's no beating this guy.

After two fairly easy cuts, we're on our way again, but are stopped by a jumble of fallen trees I'd describe as an avalanche. So we leave our bikes there, and start walking.

It's an uphill climb, and it curves 90 degrees to the left, just as Dave expected, paralleling the lower road. That's good news, since we're now headed towards the probable position of 2-Trees, but above the lower slash.

At a nondescript turnout in the old road which I probably would have missed, Dave says: "This is where they plan to reactivate this area for logging. There'll be a new road headed up there, right towards your trees."

How he knows this I don't know. But I have no doubt there will be a new logging road here in the near future.

"That would be great," I reply. "Rather than have to hike through the mess between here and the ridge, I'll be able to drive right to my goal."

"Maybe. If you wait long enough."

We both know we'd rather find the trees now than a year or more from now. But it won't be today.

We continue hiking to the end of the road, where we look up to another (but smaller) slash that heads towards the ridge. 2-Trees could be up there, no more than 200 metres away.

The day is dwindling, and we still need to drive back to the barge, and then back down the lake (and then back up the lake to my cabin). So we won't find the two old-growth beauties today. But there will be other days.

Or maybe I'll just wait for the new road, and drive right to 2-Trees.

Chapter 10

Cutting My Way Through
Chippewa North

On a mid-February Sunday, foggy morning skies are forecast to break into sunny conditions. Recent weeks have been unseasonably warm but wet, so the expectation of clearing is a welcome relief. Our quads have sat inactive on the barge for over a month, but today should be a good opportunity to get riding again.

As the sun begins to break through, we pack the barge for a day-trip to Goat Island or maybe Olsen's Landing. Where we go is unimportant. Just getting out and about is the essential part, so we leave without a specific destination. Our plan is to cruise past Goat Island's Clover Dock first, to see if any logging activity is evident. Even though this is a Sunday, Goat Island has been the focus for a lot of harvesting and some lingering road-building lately, so work may be in progress even on a weekend.

As we approach Elvis Point, Margy drives the barge while I begin off-load preparation on the deck for whatever barge ramp awaits us today. We'll know about Clover Dock when we come around the corner in a few minutes.

While unstrapping my quad, the sudden reduction of the barge's throttle grabs my attention, and I stumble in surprise. I look towards the front, and see a 5-metre log right off the bow, oriented perfectly broadside to the boat. No sooner do I see the log than it hits the barge: *Wham!*

I hear the log rolling under the boat, rubbing against the bottom. It will be only a few seconds before it reaches the leg of the outboard motor, and I expect it to be a direct hit. The good news is the barge has now slowed to a crawl, the result of Margy's quick reduction on the throttle. The even better news is I feel a final bump as the log bounces near the stern, and then all is quiet. It has skipped below and behind the motor's skeg, without impact.

When I get back to the cab, Margy is upset, but similarly thrilled we dodged this bullet.

"I didn't hear it hit the skeg, did you?" I ask.

"I think it somehow cleared the leg completely," replies Margy, with an obvious sense of relief.

"Tough boat!" I remark. "But that was a mighty big log."

"Didn't even see it until it was right on top of us," replies Margy. "I was watching you when I should have been watching for logs."

The lake has been high the past few weeks, a direct result of the heavy and nearly continuous rain. High water pulls logs from the shore, creating a boating hazard, but Margy tends to be especially attentive to such conditions. Today, she let her guard down for just an instant. That's all it takes.

We laugh it off, knowing we're fortunate the outboard motor survived this encounter without any damage. Margy pushes the throttle up again, both of us now in a more observant mode, scanning for logs and the first sign of activity at the dock. Rounding the point, sure enough, there sits *Road Cruise*, along with another crew boat. This isn't a good day to go riding on Goat Island.

"Let's go to Olsen's," I suggest, and Margy immediately turns northward.

"Or there's Chip North, right across from us," replies Margy.

From Clover Dock, Chippewa North is an obvious landmark on the opposite side of the lake, now only a few klicks away. This is an area we've never ridden, although we've talked about it a lot. Unfortunately, there are two problems with this destination: first, the dock has been in shambles for several years; and second, the climb may be too steep for Margy's comfort. But I'm thrilled Margy has suggested this spot, since it's a place near the top of my to-do list.

"Let's go!" I respond, wanting to take advantage of the proposal before Margy changes her mind.

Within just a few minutes, I'm on the deck making final preparations for our arrival. The shoreline beyond Chip North is a steep slope covered by low stratus clouds that have risen above lake-level after the morning's fog. The top of the high, long ridge is hidden within the overcast.

As we get closer, it's obvious that the dock is still a mess, broken lose from shore, and not a good place to tie-up for the day. We'll need to wade to shore from the dock, but there's a solution.

"What do you think?" I ask Margy, after returning to the cab before she pulls into the barge ramp.

"Nobody's coming here today," she replies. "No boats at the dock, so no logging or road-building. I'd be comfortable tying up at the barge ramp. We won't be blocking anyone."

We try to be good recreational partners with others, but this is becoming a more acceptable solution over time. Besides, this ramp is

Approaching Chip North

particularly wide, so we can tie-up to one side, in case anyone arrives while we're riding. We're into our second year of barging on the lake, and so far we've never encountered another landing craft or barge at any of the lake's ramps. At an inactive spot like this, it's especially unlikely. So we off-load, and then push-and-pole our barge to the side of the ramp, tying it securely in case winds develop while we're gone.

We begin our ride on the low road, which arcs off to the north from the barge ramp. The logging main ends in a slash, so we turn around to try the upper road. But it doesn't take long for Margy to realize this isn't going to work for her.

"I'm starting to freeze up," she says when I pull up next to her at a turnout.

"No sense pushing it. Do you feel okay about my trying the upper road without you?" I ask.

"Of course," she responds. "I brought along a book, and I'd like to explore around the barge for some photos of plants. Take your time."

Barge Ramp at Chip North

I pull out our walkie-talkies, and we test them.

"I'll check in with you along the way, but I may be out of range if I crest the hill."

"No problem," replies Margy. "I'll be fine."

"Here, take the bear spray, just in case," I say, handing her the canister.

I'm lucky Margy is the independent soul that she is, always ready to assume responsibility for herself, and never worried about being alone in the bush in conditions like this. It's obvious she should keep the bear spray, since she'll be more exposed than me. So I don't hesitate to suggest things that might remind her of the inherent dangers of being alone in the wilderness. We make a good team, both together and apart.

Before climbing the steeper route, I first divert off to the south, to drive above the floating cabin that's poised below a field of giant boulders. I recall this cabin owner asking Mike, a Western Forest Products representative, about these boulders at our last Powell Lake Cabin Owners' Association meeting. The cabin owner noted his wife was worried about the giant rocks, and they certainly look precarious when you view them from near the cabin at water level. Mike reassured him that the area was surveyed for stability when they finished logging on Chip North a few years ago. Still, when these cabin occupants look up from their cabin, it must be an intimidating sight, with one particularly giant boulder hanging precipitously on the steep slope above.

I drive as far as I can go, which takes me right into the boulder field. The road ends near a tumbling creek that's creating it's own miniature fog bank from the spraying water. I stop to survey the amazing sight – huge glacial erratics suspended on a slope that's close to the maximum angle of repose. If the incline were any steeper, the whole mountain would tumble down, with or without the boulders.

I return to the junction with the upper road, and turn uphill to begin the climb. It's a beautiful old main with awesome views looking down on Powell Lake. I catch a glimpse of our barge far below, now just a tiny but distinct object in the distance.

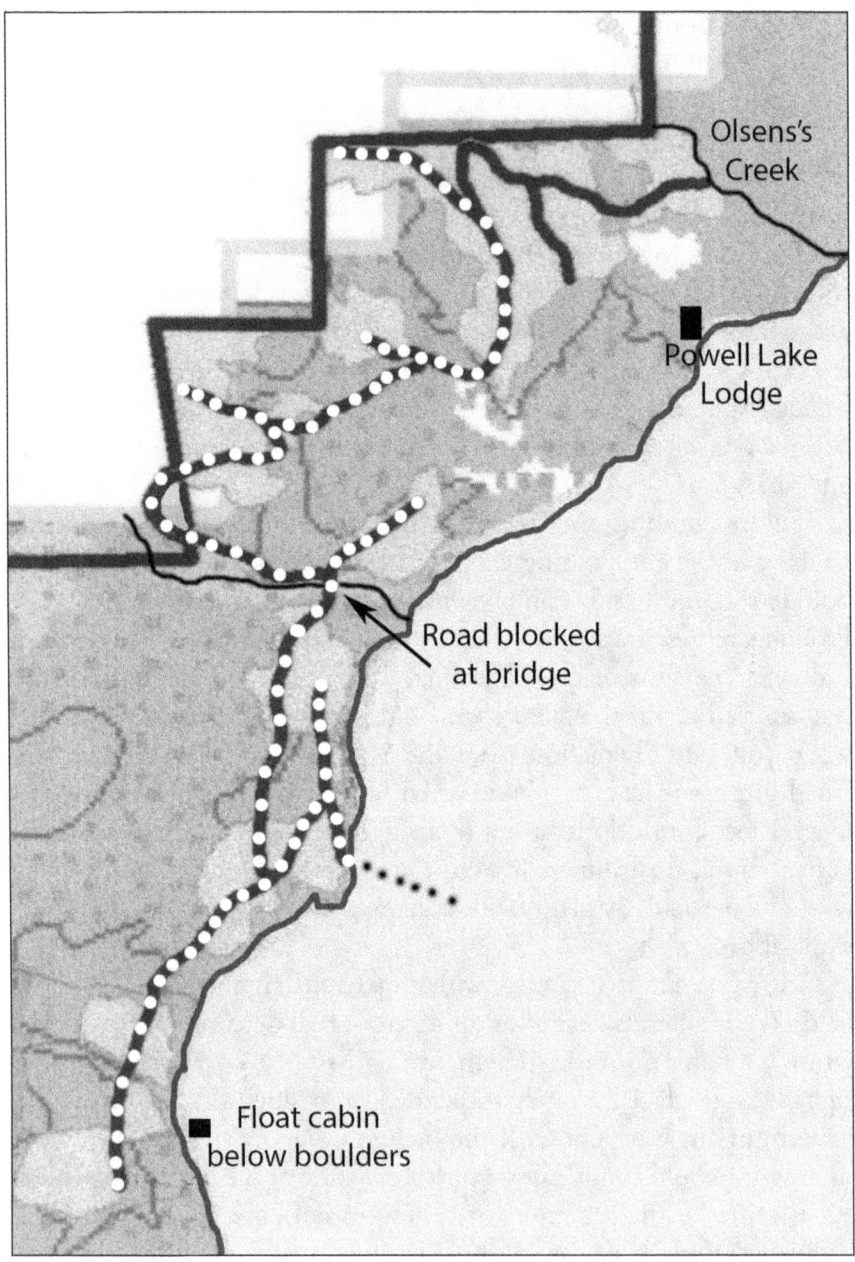

Chip North

No one has been on this road for many months, as evidenced by the numerous logs that have blown down and now obstruct the route. At some spots, I can drive over logs of small girth, since the undercarriage of my quad is designed for the task. At other locations, I get off my bike and pull branches to the side far enough to open up a clear passage. But in several places, logs completely block the road, so I need to chainsaw my way through.

As I approach a major bridge, a particularly large log blocks my path. I stop and walk over the uprooted blow-down and across the bridge, to see if there are other obstructions ahead. In conditions like this, it can be a never-ending process.

In this case, I walk to the junction on the other side of the bridge, where I can see in both directions for quite a distance. No logs here, so I return to the bridge and begin to cut. But first I check in with Margy on the walkie-talkie.

"After I cut this log, I'll be headed over the ridge, so my transmissions may be blocked until I return to this spot. I'll make sure I don't go any longer than twenty minutes before turning around. So that's forty minutes round-trip, plus an extra ten for clearing this log first. I'll call it an hour."

"I'm doing fine," replies Margy. "I've found lots of plants to study along the road near the barge. Having fun."

Log Blocking Road at Chip North

I finish cutting the log near the bridge, and then climb upwards towards the ridge that nearly connects to Olsen's Landing. I don't plan to go to the end today, but I'd like to get high enough to get a clear view to the north, maybe even looking down on Olsen Valley.

The road continues to wind upward, and then it's clear I've crossed the ridge and am starting down. I need to stop several times for brief cuts of small logs and branches, but I keep a close eye on my watch to make sure I don't exceed the timeline I've promised Margy.

I have enough time to investigate all of the short spurs that lead to dead ends in slashes. Each is different, and it's an enjoyable exploration, knowing I'm the first person through here in many months, probably since last summer. Finally, I stop at a spur that looks down on a major junction that splits towards Olsen's Creek (out of sight beyond the trees) and down to the shore near Powell Lake Resort, the old cabins that have been unoccupied for several years.

I've ridden far enough, and it's time to turn around and make walkie-talkie contact with Margy. I pause at this overlook long enough to think about how wonderful it is to ride a remote road you know no one has been on in a very long time. It's a feeling of privilege few people experience in their lifetime. And I'm grateful to be here on this February afternoon.

Chapter 11

A Touch of Summer
Olsen's Landing

APRIL BRINGS A BEAUTIFUL SPURT OF SUNSHINE AND WARMTH. Winter was particularly mild, with little snow in the high country, which doesn't bode well for the coming summer. Drinking water reserves are plentiful here, even in the driest months, but several years in a row of reduced snowpack will take its toll. Worse, the fire season looms critical this year, so logging companies are working long hours in the spring in anticipation of a summer shutdown. In my memory, dating back to my first visits here over 15 years ago, I recall no drier winter.

For those of us who use the lake for recreation, it's a wonderful April, full of opportunities to gather some pre-summer sun and explore the backcountry. Margy and I are quick to take advantage of what's advertised as one of the last days of bright April sunshine, with a spring storm forecast to move through the region tomorrow.

We load up the barge, packing the aft boxes of our quads for a day-trip. We'll head north, first checking out Goat Island's Clover Dock, although we expect logging activity to be in progress. If crew boats are parked at Clover, we'll continue north to Olsen's Landing, which has become a common scenario. Try this, or then this. When we're traveling to a quad destination, just cruising in our barge is at least half the fun.

Olsen's Landing is a different forestry jurisdiction than the lands logged by Western Forest Products, so we depart Hole in the Wall with no information about logging activity there. But Olsen's has been inactive for over a year now, and we don't expect to find any crew boats at the dock.

As we begin the trip north, the lake is perfectly still, with bold reflections in the water from the mountains that drop nearly vertically on both sides of the lake. The sun is bright and summer-like, with temperatures warm enough to send me outside onto the catwalk, reaching back inside the cab every few minutes to adjust the steering wheel. Meanwhile, Margy sits on a cushion in the other open doorway, absorbing the scenery. This touch of summer is a welcome relief, with short days falling behind us now.

I leave the quads fully tied down, waiting until we're sure where we'll off-load. As usual, we'll know for sure about Goat Island when we round the promontory where a log boom is tied up near the logging dock.

"If we see any boats at Clover Dock we'll just keep going to Olsen's," suggests Margy as we approach the boom.

"Sure. Olsen's will be fine," I reply.

"And then, if Olsen's is busy, we can come back to Chip North," adds Margy.

Northbound Towards Olsen's Landing

"As far as I'm concerned, if Olsen's is busy, we can just motor down the other side of the lake, and go home," I comment. "Heck, I don't even care if we ride our quads today. It's just fun to be out in the barge."

Which is exactly the point. This boat has been a huge success. We enjoy every aspect of it, including just cruising around and enjoying the slow pace. Sure, it transports our quads to great adventures, but voyaging in the barge is a thrill in itself. Especially on a sunny, near-summer day.

The log boom ahead continues beyond the headland, joined to an extended mass of even more logs tied together around the corner. Clover Dock itself confirms what we expect. Two crew boats are tied up, a sidewinder floats nearby, and a temporary blue canopy has been erected at the log dump. All are signs of active logging. So we pull in close for a better look (Lookie-Loo's!), and then veer off to the north.

We slide along the shore, passing a cabin with smoke pouring from the chimney, a sure sign of occupancy on a relatively unoccupied lake. Just beyond this cabin, a boat is tied to a float cabin, but nobody seems to be around. Sometimes, cabin owners store boats at their cabins during the off-season. Considering the beauty of this summer-like

Goat Island Clover Dock

day, it's surprising that so few owners occupy their recreational homes today.

We pass the cabin where a small waterfall from Clover Lake tumbles down into Powell Lake.

"Lots of water today, which kinda' surprises me," I note to Margy. By mid-summer, this flow of water will likely drop to a trickle, based on the current snowpack conditions.

This upper portion of Powell Lake is seldom as calm as we find it today. Reflections of the glacier-covered summits spread towards us from the north. These glaciers have become gradually depleted in recent years, but this year's April view is particularly disturbing. Dirty cream-coloured granite rather than white snowpack covers most of the high peaks.

In the calm water, the barge seems to propel itself faster than normal. I navigate to the opposite shore, tracking towards the white point on the water that I know is the *Mugwump*, parked at the Powell Lake Resort, a remote retreat unoccupied in recent years.

Beartooth Reflections

Approaching the old boat, we find it listing slightly to the starboard, filling with water during the wet months, probably fighting a bilge pump that relies on a depleted battery. Every time I see this familiar boat, I'm reminded of how I almost bought it over a decade ago.

"We were almost the proud owners of the *Mugwump*," I remind Margy as we pass.

"What a problem that would have been," she remarks.

"Especially when you try to picture *Mugwump* floating in the ocean," I add, which is where we had planned to use the boat in a fit of insanity that's best attributed to a love of boats of all kinds.

"Compare that to this barge," she says. "One great decision, compared to one that could have killed us."

Literally. The ocean is an unforgiving environment.

Beyond the resort, the outlet of Olsen's Creek is a major washout. The mouth of the creek has been completely reshaped and broadened, and we inspect it with interest as we pass by on our way to the barge ramp and dock.

I still haven't untied the quads, although we're now approaching Olsen's Landing. There's no boat activity at the dock, and the water is so calm today that nothing demands hurrying. We can easily float offshore while I prepare the quads, or even wait until after we've landed. Besides, the last time we visited this area, the barge ramp was full of loose wood, and might not be usable today. There's no use going through all the steps in preparing for a landing only to button things back up and go home.

I state the obvious: "The quads aren't ready for off-load yet."

"We'll know the condition of the ramp when we get closer," notes Margy. "If you want to wait until we're grounded on the beach, that's okay with me."

"Good. Let's do it that way. There's absolutely no wind to deal with."

Wind is always our biggest challenge during arrival at a barge ramp. And Olsen's Landing is a place where wind is always expected. But not today.

By the time we're able to verify that the beach is usable (although lots of wood remains along the shore), we're already set up for a nice approach. So we continue in, tilting the motor upward as the water shallows, glancing back to assure there's plenty of cooling water pumping from the outlet in the leg.

We grind to a gentle halt in the fine gravel. The stern doesn't swing even a bit to either side, evidence of the calm conditions.

We take our time getting set up for the off-load of our quads, first extending our metal ramps, which nicely overlay a big log that lies along shore. We'll be able to drive our bikes off the barge, right over the log, and then down onto a mat of smaller wood. It's an easy off-load and a simple tie-up to huge logs off to each side.

There's another, smaller barge ramp between here and the dock. It's clogged with small logs today, but could be easily cleared, if anyone else needs it today. So here's another case where we'll forego the extra time involved in moving the barge to-and-from the dock.

We've talked about riding the lower road that extends northward along the shore, a route we've scrutinized by boat previously. From just offshore, the road seems in good condition, but I've heard it's barely passible because of overgrown conditions.

Margy at Olsen's Landing

Margy leads us up to the first right turn, which might be the entry to the northbound road, but it quickly proves to be a dead end. So she turns around, and we continue farther up Olsen's Main until another trail peels off to our right. This time, we head towards the correct entry to the northbound old logging road. I take the lead now, and it's a wonderful ride that's relatively unhindered by overgrowth.

Two grouse appear along the right side of the road, flying ahead in their typical low-level fluttering manner. One bird breaks off into the forest, but the other continues to leap-frog its way in front of me, probably diverting me away from its baby chicks. Finally, I watch it fly off awkwardly, as grouse do, towards the shore on the right, it's mission accomplished.

Just as the grouse disappears, I refocus on the road in front of me. A black bear comes almost immediately into view. It's a big bear, and I catch just a glimpse as it jumps into the bush to the right. I stop my quad and wait for Margy to catch up with me.

"Did you see the bear?" I ask.

"No. I was watching the grouse."

"Big one. Full-grown," I reply. "It jumped off the road quickly, probably frightened by our quads."

"Oh, sorry I missed it."

And I know she regrets not seeing the bear. Like me, Margy hates to miss any wildlife that pops into view as we drive. But trying to keep our attention on the road, we tend to miss a lot.

After a few more kilometres, we find the road deactivated by a deep trench with a small creek eroding the ditch even further. A culvert has been pulled out of the ground, leaving the trench as a nearly impossible obstacle. As I look it over, I conclude it might be within my capabilities to descend into the trench and out the other side, but it's not worth the risk. So I don't hesitate any longer. We turn around and head southward again.

Back on Olsen's Main, we climb past familiar territory, including turn-offs we've explored in previous years. Today, we're looking for a simple ride, so we continue until we reach the turnoff to Olsen's Lake, just past the bridge over the Theodosia River. We follow the trail that leads to the lake, our path paralleling the river. Very little water flows this year, less than I ever remember, especially during the spring.

Olsen's Lake

We stop at the lake overlook and watch the summer-like scene. As is true everywhere today, the reflections of the land and clouds in the water are overwhelming.

We relax here, sharing a cool drink, while three merganser ducks float and flap their wings lackadaisically just offshore, playing in the warm sunshine. It's another reminder that summer is on its way. Everyone and everything is ready to frolic in the warm weather.

"Do you want to continue up the main?" I ask Margy.

"Not really, but I'll keep going, if you want to go farther."

"Let's start back down, and try some of the spurs off to the side," I reply.

"Did you see the turnoff that looked like the trail to the old cabin?"

She's referring to an earlier trek with John to the old Harper cabin off the lower portion of Olsen's Main (*Farther Up the Main*, Chapter 11). On that memorable day, we raced Ernie to the treasured site. (A very competitive John judged the rivalry as a tie.)

"Sure, we can try that trail, and some of the others, too," I suggest.

This has been an easy ride so far. But we want to save enough time to load up some driftwood before we depart the barge ramp. On the way home, we'll probably troll for trout, so the day will pretty full. For most quad enthusiasts, such a short ride would be "wimpy," but we're totally satisfied combining it with an overall outing on the lake. Our barge provides us with the flexibility to do all of this in a single afternoon.

After leaving Olsen's Lake, we pull over briefly at the Theodosia Main junction where I check out the sign that reads: "Hell," with an arrow indicating the route to fire and brimstone. (Which is far from an abyss, as documented in detail in *Beyond the Main*, Chapter 13.)

From here, I lead the way down Olsen's Main, stopping at one spur that leads to the right. This may be the road to the old Harper cabin, but I motion to Margy to wait while I check the condition of the trail. After riding only a hundred metres, I recognize how overgrown this road has become, so I turn around and head back to Margy's parked quad.

"You're not going to like this," I state matter-of-factly.

"Okay, I don't need to do it then," she replies.

Just as simple as that, we turn around and rejoin Olsen's Main. There are so many wonderful places to ride on our quads that we don't need to go places where we have to battle the terrain. We're both comfortable with that concept, and it makes for easy decisions.

Continuing down the main, we pass the entrance to Dagleish Main, where we've explored on two separate occasions, including a ride the previous year until we could continue no farther due to a deep trench. There's no need to prolong our ride today, so we just keep going.

On our left, less than a kilometre beyond the Dagleish Main turnoff is an old road that seems in good condition. I turn here and start up a steep slope, and Margy follows. I continue at a fairly rapid pace, leaving Margy climbing more slowly. When I come to a nearly washed out precarious section of the road, I know Margy won't want to pass through here. But I feel comfortable, so I go a little farther.

The washout section requires an adrenaline-producing quick spurt of throttle to assure the steep downhill slope doesn't cave in from the passage of my quad. It holds firm, and I continue another klick, until a fallen tree blocks the road. I could stop and chainsaw my way through, but I've seen enough today. So I turn around, and meet Margy right where I expected to find her – waiting for me at the approach to the washout, already turned around and ready to start back down.

I use another quick burst of throttle to move quickly across the washout area, and then we descend down the old road, taking in sweeping views of Powell Lake below.

Back at the barge, after loading our quads, we linger for a while, piling driftwood along the sides of the deck, to be added to our already-growing firewood stash for next winter. When we're out-and-about in the barge, we never pass up a chance to add some wood to our firewood float, especially after our quads are already loaded and we're headed home.

When we're finally ready to go, we push the barge into deeper water, aided by reverse-thrust from the 50-horsepower outboard. Margy swings the boat around, heading for home along the shore. I ask her to drive slowly, while I toss both of our fishing lines overboard for my first try of recently-opened trout season (April 1). It takes me awhile to get our lines in the water, so Margy swings in a wide off-shore 360-degree turn to give us a full run at the mouth of Olsen's Creek.

By now, I've cranked up the kicker, and Margy has turned off the bigger engine. We troll past the usually abundant trout waters at the mouth of the creek, with not a single bite. But we're fine with that. We're glad to be out in the summer-like air, enjoying the lake we love so much.

We continue to troll all the way past the breakwater boom of Powell Lake Resort, giving the ol' *Mugwump* one last look.

"Ain't she a beauty?" I say.

"If you like old, leaky boats," laughs Margy.

Once we're past the resort, Margy cranks up the 50-horse motor again. I climb out onto the swim-grid, and turn off the kicker. I tilt it up out of the water, and we slowly barge our way home.

◊ ◊ ◊ ◊ ◊ ◊ ◊

Chapter 12

Two Chips
Chippewa South and Chippewa North

Previously, I visited Chip North and Chip South. Right after road construction was complete at Chippewa South, Margy and I rode both directions from the barge ramp under the shade of trees still standing right up to the edge of the road. Now, less than a year later, the logging company has completed their work, so the new main is easily visible during our trips up and down Powell Lake. So much investment and demanding hard work for such a short period of time and such a small cut. The loggers probably won't be back until the area greens up after at least a decade.

Chippewa North is an older and more extensive logging area, idle now for at least 5 years, and similarly left to regrow before future harvesting. Although I've ridden both Chips fairly recently, today I'll be riding with John, so who knows what might happen. Riding with John is always exciting.

We'll be heading north from the Shinglemill to Chip North, and then back down the lake to Chip South, if our plan stands. Seldom does riding with John end up progressing as planned. Which makes for unique adventures.

John's big Suzuki KingQuad will fit easily aboard our barge, but we'll need to change the floor plan for our two Kodiaks. At the Hole in the Wall the night before our ride, Margy and I jostle our quads into sideways, full aft against the cab. This leaves plenty of space for the third quad on the bow, and enough extra deck for several people and a big dog.

The next morning, we motor down the lake to meet John and Bro. At Kinsman's Beach, adjacent to the Shinglemill, Margy drives the barge towards shore, as I walk out to the bow to prepare the metal ramps. Simultaneously, John drives his quad down the beach road, headed right at us.

"Hey, you're early!" I yell to John. "You weren't supposed to be here until 9:30. It's only 9:29. Couldn't you be a bit more punctual!"

"Not bad, eh?" John yells back, as he hops off his quad.

Just as the barge grinds quietly onto one of the few sandy beaches on the entire lake, John reaches onto the deck to pull the metal ramps to shore. In just a few minutes, we're loaded and gone, Margy remaining at the helm for our departure. Meanwhile John, Bro, and I settle in on the deck, discussing our plans for the day.

Before we're halfway to Hole in the Wall, I weave my way around the quads and into the cab to join Margy.

"New plan," I say. "We'll do Chip South first, just in case the wind picks up later in the day. It can get pretty rough there when the wind blows up the lake."

"Sure," she responds. "Does John want to drive the barge?"

"Not today. He's got an ear ache, and he says it's too noisy back here."

It's extremely unusual for John not to drive when we're aboard any vehicle, and for him to let Margy maneuver the barge to and from shore seems a bit strange. He trusts us, but he's always the "Captain."

"Maybe you should take us ashore at Chip South then," Margy responds. "John might feel better about it."

"No, he's content to just ride today. So take advantage of it. Follow the shoreline close, so we can check things out."

John is forever checking things out. He's an observer of detail, and nature is where he thrives. There are a lot of trees, rocks, and driftwood along the shore today, and John inspects everything closely as we slip by.

Chip South is an easy ramp when the wind is calm like this morning, but probably not later today when typical up-lake winds argue for position where the North Sea meets Chippewa Bay. Things can change fast. Today, nature gives us a break, and we're in and out of Chip South in only an hour. The amount of riding you can do here is minimal, with only two branches of the main running in opposite directions from the barge ramp.

First, we ride the shorter spur to the north, where the road overlooks the head of Chippewa Bay, a gorgeous sight on a sunny day. With no trees along the side of the road, sweeping panoramas of Powell Lake spread below us. The nearly-calm North Sea and majestic Goat Island dominate the view, so I pause for a few minutes to take it all in and shoot another photo of a lake that has consumed my attention over the past fifteen years.

Chip South is a very brief stop today, but John has never been here before. It's a logging road that's only accessible by boat, making it even more interesting for John. The overlook on the south spur provides a majestic view of the cabins across the lake, including his own Cabin Number 5. From his cabin, over the past year-and-a-half, he's watched Western Forest Products build the new main and then log this patch of forest. Finally, he's here riding on the new road.

North Sea and Goat Island from Chip South

Our re-load of the barge is quick, and we're off for Chip North, through First Narrows, past the entrance to Hole in the Wall, and along the west shore of the lake. The wide bay near Stump Creek looks across to the logging dock at Goat Island (Clover Dock) where a lot of logging activity is currently underway. I drive the barge now, while Margy and John sit on quads on the front deck, talking up a storm. Bro is spread out in his favourite position aboard any boat – in the bow, as far forward as he can go. Walkie-talkies allow me to comfortably communicate with Margy and John.

"Hey, John, take a look at Clover Dock," I transmit over the handheld radio. "How many boats today?"

From our position on the opposite side of the lake, I can see the dock (barely), but boat-size objects are not clearly visible.

"He says there's three, all crew boats," reports Margy over the walkie-talkie.

Best eyes I've ever known. Never a match for me or anybody else.

"And there's a big log boom on the point that looks full," adds Margy over the handheld. "Busy place."

Margy and John on Barge Deck

We try to keep track of the logging activity on Goat Island, since it's one of our favourite riding destinations. After an extensive period of road construction, log hauling now has begun. When they're finished, we'll be able to return to the island with our barge during the week, rather than only on weekends.

I drive along Stump Creek, close enough to "check things out" while still clear of the big snags. We're close enough to shore that I'm not able to see around the corner to Chip North until we're almost there. So I'm surprised when I round the point and see the old dock swung around so it completely blocks the barge ramp. This dilapidated dock has been partially detached from the stairs to shore for the last two years, but today it's in total disarray. Still, I'm confident there's an easy solution, and so is John. In fact, it's almost uncanny how we immediately communicate without even using the walkie-talkies.

John waves his arm at the tip of the dock, farthest from the bridge to shore, and I immediately maneuver in that direction. I watch him reach down and pick up the pike pole, so it's obvious what he's going to try to do – grab the end of the dock so we can use the barge to pull it back into position. It's a simple plan, but it doesn't work.

Once aligned with the tip of the dock, I shift into neutral, and glide gently into position. John jabs the pike pole into the railing, and nods his head to tell me to shift into reverse. I try idle-reverse at first, but then need to rev up the engine to get some thrust. As the thrust increases, John can't hold his grip, and has to release the pike pole from the railing.

I step out onto the catwalk and lean forward.

"Now what?" I yell.

"Pull back into position, and I'll tie a rope. Not sure we can do it in reverse though. May need to switch around to use forward gear to give us more power."

"So you want to try reverse first?"

"Sure. We're already here, so let's give 'er a go."

After John secures the rope, I shift into reverse and rev up the engine a bit. There's a brief delay, and then the dock begins to swing outward, swinging nicely back towards where we want it. In just a few minutes, the old dock is back in position, looking (at least for the moment) in perfect alignment. John unties the rope, and I maneuver around to get lined up with the barge ramp.

We make another as-perfect-as-it-gets shore arrival, using our big ropes to hold the barge securely in place while we off-load. Like we did back at Chip South, we decide to leave the barge at the ramp rather than tie it to the dock (which isn't a good place to tie up anyway). Today, Margy will remain behind while John and I ride the upper road at Chip North, so there'll be no problem with others wanting to come ashore while the boat is unattended.

The plan for Margy to stay behind at the barge isn't something I look forward to explaining to John. However, Margy and I discussed it earlier in the morning. We agreed this is no place for her to ride today. John likes to explore "tough" trails, and the main here is high and precipitous, not the kind of riding environment Margy enjoys. Plus, John has already hinted there's an old trail that connects this logging complex to Theodosia, but it's a difficult route. There's no doubt John will want to try it, and John's "tough" trails are not the level of riding most riders enjoy. Margy will be content to stay behind, absorbing the warm sunshine, photographing the nearby plants and shrubs, and enjoying a good book. Telling this to John, on the other hand, is something I dread.

This is counter to one of John's credos – never leave a man (or woman) behind. In fact, that's even more closely enforced when Margy is involved. John feels very protective of her, and that's certainly not a bad thing, so leaving her behind will probably not go over well.

Strangely, when I explain our decision, John quickly agrees.

"That old trail to Theo will be quite a mess," he notes. "Haven't been through there in about two years, and I'm sure no one else has used it either. Rick and I opened it up about ten years ago, and it's pretty rough, so Margy wouldn't like it"

Two milestones in a single day: John is riding in our barge as a passenger rather than captain; and he's going to leave someone behind (although in well-controlled circumstances). We'll leave Margy with a walkie-talkie and my bear spray, and she'll be fine at the barge by herself.

* * * * *

John and I (with Bro in the aft box of the KingQuad) climb quickly up the main, looking back down on the barge. We both wave to Margy, but we're already too far away for her to see us.

We soon come to a twin-tree that's fallen across the main, but it remains high enough on one side for us to slip under with our quads.

"Was this here before?" asks John when I catch up to him to begin slowly slipping under the trees.

He knows I've recently traveled this main alone. At the time, I thought this main connected to another road just south of Olsen's Lake, but John has explained today that there's no such connection. So we'll be riding as far as the dead end, if we don't get involved in the old trail John wants to try before we get there.

"Same fallen trees as before," I answer, proud to report that I rode this path previously.

Farther up the main, as we approach the only significant bridge on the road, John slows to allow me to catch up, gesturing towards the log where I used my chainsaw to begin cutting my way through during my previous visit. I proudly nod my head in reply, and mouth the word "Yes," acknowledging it was indeed me, Mr. Mountain Man, who made this cut.

On the other side of the bridge, John stops, studying the gully to the left side. At first I don't see anything here, but then I look more closely. Beyond the ditch at the side of the road, the thick brush seems just a little thinner, marking the hint of an old trail.

"That's our trail," says John. "Rick and I re-opened an old logging road that ran all the way from Theodosia to here, and then right down to the beach."

He points towards the other side of the road, where a big fallen fir with branches of thick needles blocks our view of anything else on that side.

"That side is trashed," adds John. "But our old trail to Theo still looks pretty good. Hasn't been fully reopened for about 10 years, but I came through it again a few years ago. Quite a mess then."

"So that was before Chip North was here," I suggest.

"Nothing here 10 years ago," confirms John.

"So the bridge wasn't here either?"

"Nope. No roads, no bridges. Just a bushwhacked trail from Theo to Powell Lake."

I can imagine how difficult it would be to ride that trail today. The overgrown path in the forest will probably include fallen trees completely blocking it in many places. Who knows what else?

"Might not be so bad once you get into the bigger trees," suggests John. "The canopy protects things below."

So are we going to try this trail today? Obviously, if we do, it will be a major trail re-opening exercise just to get started, which is something John does at the drop of a hat. For me, not so much.

But John pauses here no longer. He shifts into gear, and off we go, continuing on the main I rode a few months ago, rather than across the ditch and onto the old trail. I follow John, wondering if he plans to return here later today, and flog our way into the forest. After all, we'll need to pass right by on our way back to the barge.

The rest of the ride on the main is uneventful. We slow to pass several spots where trees had fallen but I previously cleared the path with my chainsaw. No new blow-downs are present, and the overall road condition is good. We ride until the road ends, still several kilometres from Olsen's Landing. And then we backtrack to the bridge, where John stops at the spot where the old trail enters the bush. He pauses only a few seconds, and then his quad drops down into the trench and up the other side. In just moments, he vanishes, his Suzuki pushing aside the bushes, leaving a path clear for me.

I don't hesitate any longer. I follow John's quad, but within seconds, nothing but bushes surround me. The trail I'm on is completely obliterated, but I push forward a few more metres, and there's the faint outline of where John has passed. He calls it a trail. I call it thrashing into nowhere.

I catch a glimpse of John's quad ahead of me, which is reassuring. I speed up a bit in these very difficult conditions, not wanting to lose sight of him, which would mean losing sight of the trail.

I pull up behind John, where he's stopped and already off his quad and removing his chainsaw.

"Needs a little work," he says, as he performs a classic drop-start of his saw.

A few metres in front of us is an old log, fallen within the past few years since John has been through here. The fact he's cutting it means we'll probably be fighting our way through this trail all afternoon. Knowing John, it's hard to imagine turning around and going back once we've started. I have no idea how far this trail weaves towards Theodosia, but I now know I'll be seeing every bit of it today. Unless, of course, an immovable obstacle comes along, which is rare. But a total rock avalanche might save me.

We press on, and it doesn't get any easier. We drive only a short distance before John must cut through another blow-down. I too have a chainsaw on the front of my quad, but John is notoriously quick at pulling his saw into position, making a quick start, and cutting. By the time I could walk around John and get to the logs in front of him, he'd be finished. So instead, I try to catch up with him as quickly as possible and assist by hauling the cut logs off the trail. This is, of course, hard work, and soon I'm sweating profusely.

Bro, meanwhile, takes it all in stride. While John drives, he peers ahead from his aft box to see what's going on. And when they stop, Bro pokes his head forward from his box to watch John cut the logs.

Then, all of a sudden, the trail gets noticeably better. We're in the big trees now, and the canopy provides protection for the trail. We still

John Cutting Log on Trail

face fallen logs occasionally, but the bushes and ugly thorny vines are mostly gone. For now.

We drive into and out of canopied areas in fits-and-starts. John's energy is endless. And my sweat seems to be endless, too, although log hauling is the easier part of the job.

In many places we avoid cutting by driving over smaller fallen logs. However, we need to engage our differential lockers to make this possible, and that makes steering more of chore. We're close to bottoming out, but the undercarriage of a quad is amazingly tough. All of this wears us (me) down. But even for me, this is extraordinarily uplifting – pressing through a trail no one has driven in years.

In some spots, we both get off our bikes and use our garden clippers to cut our way through the thick bushes. All in all, it will be about 5 kilometres of intense work to re-open this trail.

At the far end, approaching Theodosia Valley, we face extensive muddy areas, mixed with short spurts of steep uphill terrain. Then we come to a place where two old trucks sit beside the trail. This used to

Od Trucks on Trail to Theodosia

be a logging road, and these vehicles from the 1940s are monuments to an era long ago. This far from civilization, it's like a logging museum in the middle of nowhere.

Ahead of us I see sunlight in the trees, indicating an opening in the forest. The trail gets better now, maybe indicating that quad riders have been coming in from this other side for a while now. Obviously, they didn't make it very far, as evidenced by the work needed to get through from Chip North.

We turn downhill, riding on a moss-covered trail that winds through a grove of beautiful slender trees. At our next trail-clearing stop, John explains this portion of the route is an old logging railroad, used during the days when trains were used instead of logging trucks.

There's bright light ahead now. Our trek is clearly at an end (except for the much easier return to Chip North). I'm still sweating, but with the end in sight, it's positively invigorating.

Trail building is John's thing, not mine. But I'm glad to be able to experience it, now and then, as a reminder of how lucky I am to ride the trails that have been constructed throughout this wonderful coastal region.

And some nights it's just plain exhilarating to crawl into bed exhausted, and placidly contemplate where you've been today.

Chapter 13

Secret Spot
Theodosia Valley

It's not uncommon for John to preface our rides with: "Now I don't want you writing about this." John has lots of secret spots he wants to keep to himself (and to show to a few select friends). When he invites me to a new secret spot in Theodosia Valley that he's been telling me about for several weeks, I don't need a review of the rules, but I'll hear them nevertheless.

He phones me on a Saturday morning, when the forecast is for clear skies and a high temperature of 22 degrees. Perfect riding weather.

"What are you doing today?" he asks.

"Nuttin' except for some little jobs around the cabin. What do you want to do?"

"How about you and Margy meeting me in Theo. You can take your barge to Olsen's Landing, and ride across from there. We'll go to my new secret spot."

It's an offer that's difficult to refuse, but there are complications today.

"We'd love to do that," I reply. "But Margy has come down with a cold. She can't ride today."

"That bad, eh?"

"Nothing really serious, but too much for her to ride."

"Can you handle the barge by yourself, and meet me anyway."

"The barge is no problem, but Olsen's can get pretty windy in the afternoon, and it'd be nice to have two people to bring it to shore. One for the off-load ramps and one for a pike pole in the water or at the helm to keep things under control."

"Sure," agrees John. "Olsen's does get rough most afternoons. No way to tell in advance."

"Hang on a minute…" I say, putting the phone down on the counter near the cabin's cell booster antenna, while I walk over to the couch where Margy sits, looking like death warmed over. She's heard my side of the conversation with John. Before I can say anything, she responds between coughs: "Whatever you do, be careful. Olsen's can get rough."

She gives me a knowing look that reminds me I'm about to take on a task bigger than it sounds. I walk back to the counter, and pause a moment to clear my mind before picking up the phone.

"Okay, let's do it," I tell John.

"Good. I've been hoping to take you to my secret spot. Just the three of us."

"Three? Who's the third?"

"Margy," replies John matter-of-factly. "She's not that sick, is she?"

Sometimes John only hears what he wants to hear.

"She's too sick to ride a quad or even ride with me in the barge."

"Oh. Well, okay, what time can you get there? Olsen's Lake would be a good spot to meet. If I get there first, I'll probably come on down to meet you on your way up."

"That would be good," I reply. "Let's see… I haven't even had breakfast, and I've got to gather up my gear… It'll probably be sometime between twelve-thirty and one."

"Man, I'll need to get going right away to meet you by then. But that sounds fine. Just wait at the lake if I'm not there yet. Oh, one other thing – you can't tell anyone about this spot."

"I know. Not a problem."

"They'll ruin it," says John, referring to those passer-by riders who might wreck a pristine camping spot. In this particular case, there's a deep trout pool nearby that could easily be fished out in a single day. I know the rules.

After hanging up the phone, I quickly cook myself some eggs and toast, and then pull out a checklist I use for barge trips with the quads. While I'm loading the gear at the dock, Margy struggles outside to meet me.

"I'll go with you," she states.

"No, you don't feel good enough for that."

"I won't ride my quad, but I can go with you on the barge, and help you off-load at Olsen's. There's an on-load, too. I'll just stay on the barge until you get back."

"You're too sick," I reiterate. "I'll be okay by myself."

"I know you will. But it's the same sun there as here. I may as well lay around at Olsen's Landing as here, baking this cold out of me."

She's right, and I could use her help. Margy is always self-sufficient when it comes to waiting, using the time to read and sun bathe. And it really is the same sun.

"Okay, but bring some warm clothes in case it gets cold on the barge," I say. "You know John. I might not be back until sunset."

So it's settled. We both scurry around gathering our gear, which only takes a few minutes. We're quickly underway, with Margy backing the barge out of our breakwater. At her choice, she'll handle all of the driving today, including beaching the barge and the trip home. It's therapy for a nasty ol' cold. Meanwhile, I'll take care of the deck duties.

We haven't ridden in nearly a month, so my quad needs some preparation as we cruise north. I'm happy working out in the open on the front deck, moving gear around. And Margy's inside the cab, and out of the wind (which bothers her cold-sensitive ears).

On the way north, towering cumulus clouds bloom in front of a bright-blue sky canopy. It's a glorious June day.

I've brought along a black plastic bin containing my quad gear, so first I transfer most of it to my aft-mounted box, and strap a few items onto the front rack for easy access. I hook up my portable GPS, and take a mental inventory of all I'll need today: lunch, camera, fishing gear, jacket and gloves, helmet and goggles, walkie-talkie (with one left in the barge cab for Margy), bear spray... It's a long list, but a familiar one.

The water remains fairly calm, so I begin unstrapping my quad while Margy angles from Goat Island towards Olsen's Landing. We pass the *Mugwump*, anchored at the dying Powell Lake Resort, while I consider whether I should try to jostle my quad out of its sideways position on the barge. My bike has been parked this way since our last ride, which involved three quads and a need to angle mine sideways. For now, I decide to leave my quad as it is, tucked in perpendicular, since Margy can't drive the barge and help me move my bike at the same time. Once our metal off-load ramps are deployed and we're steady in our spot, we'll have plenty of time for repositioning the sideways quad.

Margy drives us up onto the beach, and I quickly attach the metal ramps to the bow. We're firmly stabilized now, and Margy comes out of the cab to help with the off-load. Her strength is minimal today, but her assistance is valuable as I jockey the rear of my quad around in short jolts, straightening it so I can drive it off. Margy repositions the handlebars as I lift from the rear, and in three quick, short lifts, the bike is straight enough to back off the barge.

My quad is quickly off-loaded, and I park it off to the side. I retract the ramps and shove them back onto the deck. One big push from me, and we're floating again. I hop aboard the bow, as Margy backs away from the shore and motors over to the adjacent dock. We tie up the barge, do a quick test of our walkie-talkies, and I'm on my way.

* * * * *

ON THE WAY UP OLSEN'S MAIN, I'm on the lookout for bears. Bears are often seen here, and today there's plenty of scat in the middle of the road to verify their nearby presence. However, during my uphill climb, I don't see any wildlife except for numerous grouse. (That evening, on the way back down Olsen's Main, I'll see a fully-grown black bear jogging down the logging road in front of me. He continues for several hundred metres, my bike now running at reduced throttle as I follow far enough behind so I don't scare him further. Then he finds a comfortable spot to exit the main, and shuffles off into the bushes.)

I cross the bridge over Theodosia River, which flows into Olsen's Lake. On the other side of the overpass, I turn left, and descend down the trail to the lake. At the bottom of the path, where the river normally forms a wide inlet, there's almost no water. All is dry except for small puddles that indicate some underground seepage, another sign of one of the driest years on record. Scary dry, with familiar local glaciers melting and normally snow-capped peaks covered in a mix of green and granite.

I front of me, John sits on his quad, with Bro in his aft box. Both of them are gazing out at Olsen's Lake, one of the most picturesque spots in the region. The blue sky and bright white cumulus always make the sky look so huge here.

I pull up beside John, turn off my engine, and remove my helmet.

"Fancy meeting you here," I say.

"Funny place to meet. Pretty spot though."

He's beaten me here by only a few minutes, which is pretty good timing for people coming from distant departure points, using completely different routes and modes of transportation (barge and quad versus truck and quad).

From here, we start up the logging road towards Theodosia Valley, but John has some advice first.

"You'll need to stay way behind me today. Lots of dust. But I'll stop and wait for you at any intersection where it isn't obvious which way to go."

"Good," is my simple reply.

But in the back of my mind, I remember an instance (actually, several instances) years ago when I first started riding with John. On one occasion, I remember losing John in front of me, and coming to an intersection where I had to decide which way to turn. I went the wrong way. Finally, I backtracked and found John, and was chastised for my inability to know the difference between a "main" and a "spur." Somehow, today's instruction about stopping at obvious intersections seems riddled with a potential repeat performance. But before I can think it through, John is gone. So I shift into gear, and follow at a slow enough speed to let his cloud of dust disperse in front of me.

We ride on a major logging road towards Theodosia until a (somewhat) major road splits off to my left. John isn't waiting here, so I continue on what I'm sure is the main. Then I come to a 90-degree T-intersection. It's fifty-fifty which road I should take, and John isn't here either. Somehow the road to the left seems headed more directly towards Theodosia, so I start up it. But after about a kilometre, it winds back towards Powell Lake, which isn't where we're supposed to be going.

So I turn around, and backtrack to the T-intersection. I wait a few minutes, hoping John will return to find me. Then, when John doesn't appear after a few minutes, I reverse course, and head back to the seemingly obvious wrong route that angled off the main. I ride up it a few hundred metres, until it feels like it's narrowing into a dead end at a logging slash. Again, I turn around, and ride back to the T-intersection, stop, turn off my engine, and listen for John's quad. Nothing.

I'm not lost. I can backtrack to the barge, if necessary, following my GPS track to be sure I don't get off course. But where is John, and why didn't he wait for me at the T?

While I wait, I pull out my author's notebook, and begin to jot some notes about today's ride. If John never returns, it'll still make a good chapter.

Then I hear an engine that sounds like a quad. Surely it's John, coming back to find me.

When he pulls up next to me, John sees me writing in my notebook.

"Put that away!" he directs. "Don't say a word about my secret spot. I don't want the world knowing where it is."

"You know I won't do anything to identify it," I reply. "Don't I always help you keep your secrets?"

"Okay. But this one isn't just secret. It's top secret."

A highly classified destination, with more secrecy than the latest U.S. stealth bomber.

"I thought you were going to wait for me at any intersection that wasn't obvious," I retort.

"Sure. But this intersection is obvious. You have to go to the right, since it's the direction of the main road. The road to the left is a dead end."

"And how was I supposed to know that?" I ask disagreeably.

"Well, look at the tire tracks. Most of them go to the right."

Case closed. And at least I'm not lost, and we're reunited.

From here, the ride is fairly short, with several intersections (where John waits patiently for me), and finally a turn off onto a nearly invisible trail. In fact, it's intentionally unmarked to the extent that we stop right after entering. John walks back to the road, finds a small branch lying off to the side, and drags it across our tire tracks at the entrance. Just like in the cowboy movies – cover your horse's tracks behind you. Top secret.

Now the riding gets more challenging, a narrow trail that's rutted and challenging. Finally, it angles down a steep slope where John raises his hand, signaling back to me with four fingers – 4-wheel drive. I'm already in low gear and 4-wheeling, so I simply follow him carefully down to a muddy shore.

From here, we ride upstream alongside a very shallow creek, another victim of minimal snow-melt this year. Then John pulls away from the stream, back into the woods for a short stretch, until we finally come to his secret spot. (If John is reading this, he'll be laughing. Not only have I disguised it well, there are a few obvious misdirections. Tell me I can't keep a secret!).

John has manicured this secret spot in recent weeks. Like other places he's helped develop in the region, it could be a national park campground, beautifully landscaped, with a rock BBQ pit and log seats (with wooden backs). But without that man-made look. It's a natural oasis in the forest, next to a deep pool where trout swim within easy sight.

The secret spot comes complete with a forest warden – John himself. He doesn't want anyone damaging the natural beauty, and he keeps it secret to prevent others from overfishing the deep pool.

"The fish here are real easy to catch," he says. "But I prefer to just sit on the bank and watch them. Even if you try to catch-and-release, they tend to bite so hard they swallow the hook."

You can damage these trout beyond the survival point, so John's rule is that catches should be no more than the number of fish to be eaten on-site. Why should this pool of fish be decimated for future meals at home? John makes rules not everyone finds easy to follow. But they make perfect sense in a world that should be preserved for the good of all.

I'm allowed to try a few casts into the pool, but when I almost immediately hook a big trout, he says: "That's enough for today. We'll cook him up, and there's plenty for two. No sense killing more if we're not going to eat them."

So we walk back to the park-like campsite, and cook up the fish on a middle-of-nowhere BBQ. Simply delicious.

And secret spots are kept secret.

Cooking Trout at Secret Spot

Chapter 14

Summer Traffic on Goat Main
Head of Goat Lake and No Name

IF YOU LEAVE POWELL LAKE by winding through Goat River and then into Goat Lake, No Name barge ramp appears a kilometre farther up on the left-hand shore. It has intrigued me ever since I first heard its name, a place that just begs to be visited.

However, I don't expect to find much, partly because it has no dock or log skid – only a ramp leading to a deactivated road back towards Narrows to the south and the beginning of a short main to the north. John and I rode here years ago on 100 cc motorbikes, as a quick side trip in our travels from the Narrows barge ramp. Last year, Margy and I rode our quads near here during a trip from Narrows, but were stopped by a washed-out (or pulled-out) bridge crossing. When the main came to an abrupt end, I estimated we were less than a kilometre from No Name. Ever since, I've wanted to return to this unnamed location to connect back to the missing bridge site, no matter how short the ride might be. Plus, reliving more old memories, the logging road winds farther north along the Goat Lake shoreline, eventually ending at a place where John and I followed a bear who insisted on remaining on the road in front of us for at least a kilometre (*Up the Main*, Chapter 20).

Today, we'll be coasting past this area on a camping trip to the Head of Goat Lake, planning to return to No Name for an expectedly short quad ride during our voyage home. First, however, we must negotiate Goat River at a water level as low as we'll ever want to navigate. In fact, one reason we're going to Goat Lake this weekend is because we're concerned that summer lake levels are heading downward, and this will probably be our last chance to use the river route this year.

As I slowly drive the barge up Goat River, Margy climbs out onto the bow, looking for shallow water, rocks, and sunken logs. Our outboard motor is raised as high as it will safely go and still pump vital cooling water out in a pencil-thin stream. My hand rests on the throttle, ready to shift into neutral at the slightest sound of the leg hitting something or worried hand signals from Margy. For now, her hands rest at her sides, only occasionally reaching up to direct me left or right and then straight ahead again.

Successfully out of the river, the fjord-like cliffs surrounding Goat Lake immediately absorb me. Margy comes back to take over the helm, while I lengthen the tow rope for the tin boat, which has followed only a few metres behind the stern during our passage through the narrow river. She pushes the throttle up to cruising speed, and I go out to my lawn chair on the bow to enjoy the sun and watch for No Name. What a wonderful way to bask in the hot July sunshine, with a cooling 6-knot breeze created by the barge traveling at cruise speed.

Goat River

No Name appears off our left, and I examine it closely as we pass. The ramp appears clear, and the first small stretch of the road can be seen angling up from shore. From here, it's impossible to tell if the road is clear enough to ride. We may be stopped before the first bend where the dirt road goes out of sight. In fact, on our return from the Head of Goat Lake, we may land here, only to leave our quads aboard while we walk to the first turn to check it out, and find that riding is futile. Over the ten years since loggers left, nature easily may have reclaimed the clear path John and I once rode.

We cruise slowly up Goat Lake, past No Name, finding no other boats along the way. We count off the part-time cabins – three floating and two on land, and finally arrive at the barge ramp at the head of the lake.

The landing area is wide enough that we decide to off-load in the middle and then push the barge a few metres to the side. There we'll use our extended metal ramps for support, and tie up to a big log grounded at a 90-degree angle to the shore to serve as a makeshift dock.

Head of Goat Lake

It's still too hot at 2 o'clock to set up our tent, so we head for the nearby sandy beach that's only here because of the low water level. We set up our lawn chairs, and Margy pours me a welcoming Coke, complete with ice cubes, part of our tradition upon campsite arrival (or overnight anchorage) on hot summer days. We settle in for a few hours of lazy reading, and I nearly dose off in the comfortable shade.

But after two hours, the sun begins to encroach into our retreat, so we move our chairs to nearby Goat Main, where I've reconnoitered a shady bend in the road. A small turnout allows us to sit safely off the main and watch as traffic passes by.

Of course, we're not expecting much traffic. Over the next few hours, two trucks and five quads pass by, although the last two quads are John and his friend, Mike. We expected John, since he planned to meet us here, like we often meet in remote places when we travel. On the other hand, the trucks and the other three quads (which arrive first) stop to see why we're sitting here beside a dirt road in the middle of nowhere.

The two trucks are together, and the first driver pulls up next to our folding chairs, rolls down his window, and inquires why we're here.

"Funny place to find people sitting beside the road," says the driver, while his passenger leans over to see what we're doing. Meanwhile, three inquisitive big dogs jump up and down in the bed of the pickup.

"Selling cold lemonade. Fifty dollars a glass," I announce matter-of-factly.

"We'll take two!" laughs the driver.

Soon after the trucks depart, two quads slow as they approach us, and then stop and turn off their engines. I wait for them to remove their helmets so they can hear me.

"Ice cold lemonade," I announce. "Fifty bucks a glass."

"You're kind of buckling under the pressure out here, aren't you?" replies the quad rider nearest to me.

We talk for a few minutes, and then they head down the main, one of the drivers reminding me as he leaves: "You'd better relax, if you can. Don't want you stressed out too much."

A half hour later, a solo rider, headed down the main towards town pulls to a halt beside us. At first I don't recognize him. Then he pulls his helmet off, starts talking, and I realize this is Jimmy, one of John's friends.

"I left John and Mike up the main when they decided to hike over to the Eldred River for a swim," he says nonchalantly, as if he's not surprised to find people he knows sitting along Goat Main in the middle of nowhere. Maybe John told him to expect us. Then again, maybe not.

"They just keep stopping and exploring, and then they ride some more," he continues. "It's too hot for me, so I'm headed home."

"You do just fine," I reply, reminding myself Jimmy is the oldest quad rider I know, and still looking good.

"Eighty-eight, and still doing okay," he replies. "My father died at ninety, but that was in a car accident. Until then, he never saw a doctor, except a dentist, for anything."

"Good genes," says Margy, and she means it. Her mother, too, had good genes, living nearly to a hundred. Both Margy and I marvel at how much younger we feel by living outdoors as much as possible. Barge trips and quads help.

"Saw a mountain lion at about the 32 milepost, where the cliff is reinforced," says Jimmy. "Big one, with a huge tail. And then a little ways farther up the main I saw two fawns alone in the road without their mother. Seemed unusual. Maybe they were looking for their mom."

It was a sad analysis of what might have occurred. But life in the forest can be brutal. The forces of nature are not always easy to accept, but the chain of life must go on.

"Is there still a locked gate at Dianne Main?" I ask Jimmy.

Logging was very active during our visit here last summer, and we weren't able to ride Dianne Main due to the helicopter logging in progress (Chapter 2). Maybe this year, we'll be able to ride this famous road.

"No gate," says Jimmy. "But they've removed the bridge."

I try to imagine how a logging company could have accomplished this, although they remove bridges routinely after they're done logging in some areas. The bridge over the Eldred River at the beginning of Dianne Main is huge!

Jimmy departs, and an hour later, Mike arrives, followed a few minutes later (a dust length) by John. As usual, no matter where I go, John is everywhere.

We talk for a short while, and then it's time for them to head back to their trucks near Tin Hat Junction, and back to town. After they leave, the road is quiet for the rest of the evening, after this miniature traffic jam to remember.

* * * * *

As evening approaches, we're prepared to listen for splashes at night, as Sasquatch throws rocks into the water near our tent like last summer (Chapter 2). But this time the results are different. Yes, there are splashes at night, but the "rocks" as smaller. In fact, we conclude that maybe it's not Sasquatch after all. There's constant degassing of the shallow water at the head of this lake, and it's audible in calm conditions in the middle of the night. Or maybe it's frogs or small fish jumping. In any case, the big splashing of Sasquatch rocks is missing.

However, in the morning, Margy shows me clearly visible tracks of a bear that came down near our barge, within ten metres of our tent. Even so, we sleep comfortably during both nights of our stay. John says bears won't cross a small bridge, and our loading ramps are bridge-like in their design.

(Yet, we're convinced that a bear recently made an early morning visit to our float cabin. To get there, it must have crossed our narrow wooden bridge from shore. A sudden crashing sound near our parked barge woke us up, and when Margy got downstairs (quickly), she saw a bear climbing nearly straight up the nearby cliff. In any case, we're considerably less fearful of bears than cougars or even Sasquatch.)

* * * * *

We plan to spend the weekend lounging around the campsite, fishing from our tin boat, and quad riding up the main to its end at Squirrel Creek, another spot where the logging company has removed a bridge. On our way up Goat Main, we'll stop to fish in the Eldred River that parallels our course. (Except for one small trout caught fishing from shore on the Eldred River this weekend, I can't brag about the fishing. John always tells me about the two and three-pounders he catches in remote places. I refer to most of my catches as "McDonalds quarter-pounders.")

Our quad ride takes us up Goat Main past the high cliffs where rock climbers focus their energy. Near milepost 32, we pass the retainer wall where Jimmy saw the cougar, but all is quiet. After a snack stop at the spot where the bridge was removed at Squirrel Creek, we backtrack to Dianne Main. We approach the Eldred River expecting to find that bridge missing, too (per Jimmy), but the span looks fine, so we carefully cross over.

"Must be a different bridge," I say to Margy when I catch up to her on the other side. "Maybe Jimmy was talking about another bridge farther up the main that's been removed."

We start up Dianne Main, marveling at the beauty of the high mountains surrounding us. There are spots on the precipitous peaks where heli-logging has left small clear cuts. How helicopters were able to conquer this region is hard to imagine. Yet, they did it only last year. It must have been amazing to watch.

After a few kilometres, with some fairly large and deep trenches that don't stop us, we're brought to a halt by the remains of a big

Dianne Main Bridge

metal bridge that's been removed from picturesque Dianne Creek. Sections of the bridge sits partly alongside the road and partly across it, blocking our path. Removing this bridge, although smaller than the structure spanning the Eldred River, was no small feat. It now sits here ready to go back into place when logging resumes again, or to be hauled to another main in the region.

When we began today's ride, we expected it to be a fairly wimpy trip, especially with all the heat. But, instead, it turns out to be one of our longer journeys. The temperature seems cooler than expected, and we're enjoying ourselves.

Returning back down Dianne Main, I lead Margy to the turnoff for D-Branch. This is a trail she's never ridden, and I haven't been here myself in many years (*Farther Up the Main*, Chapter 2). I suspect this will be a trail that will challenge Margy to the fullest, so I'm surprised when she climbs it without hesitation. The ravine to our left falls off precipitously, with just a row of bushes along the side of the old main that provides a false sense that everything is normal. As Margy leads me up the trail, it's obvious she knows the steep gorge is immediately to our left, but she just keeps climbing.

We're slowed, but not stopped, by the first of the original avalanches John and his friends smoothed over in years gone by. I ride Margy's bike through two tough sections, and then we're on the march again. Finally, at the site of the second old avalanche, we make it through most of this section, before Margy rolls to a stop. When I catch up with her she yells back over her shoulder.

"That's it!" she announces. "Can't go any farther."

"No problem," I reply, glad we've made it this far.

"How far to Spray Creek?" she asks.

She's referring to the errant creek where Doug and I stayed behind rather than try to exit D-Branch when the water level rose with snowmelt at the end of a warm summer day. We camped overnight without sleeping bags, tent, or any overnight equipment – quite an adventure – and easily navigated Spray Creek the next morning when the flow was reduced due to colder, nighttime temperatures in the mountains above (*Farther Up the Main*, Chapter 3).

"The creek isn't much farther," I reply. "But it wouldn't look like much today. Probably almost dry this year."

We turn our quads around, and head back down D-Branch, and then down Goat Main to our barge. We're back at our campsite in time for a quiet afternoon in the sun, again lounging in our canvas chairs, enjoying the peace and tranquility of one of the most beautiful lakes in the region.

* * * * *

THE NEXT MORNING WE'RE UP EARLY, break down our tent, and load our quads back on the barge. By mid-morning, we're pulling into No Name, ready for our long awaited ride.

The barge ramp is in good shape, although unattended for years, and the lake conditions are tranquil this early in the morning, so we off-load our bikes and leave the barge positioned at the ramp.

From there, it's a short ride up to the T-intersection where the road splits to the left and right. After traveling just a few hundred metres to the left, we're stopped by the same washed-out (or removed) bridge that blocked our passage from the Narrows side last summer. In fact, on that earlier ride, we stopped within easy walking distance (if we could have crossed the creek bed) of No Name barge ramp. Yes, it has

No Name Ramp

been a bit of effort today to offload at No Name and ride such a short distance, but now I know. And I feel good about knowing.

Margy and I turn around now and ride up the main on the other side of the T-intersection. In about a kilometre, an old creek that's now dry stops us again by. This time there's no demolished (or removed) bridge, but simply a major washout from floodwater that must have roared through here during extreme storm conditions. The main is entirely impassable, but in future years, when loggers return, they'll easily get this disruption in the road fixed.

But it's too much for us to navigate today, so we turn around after less than an hour ashore at No Name, and return to the barge. It's time to navigate back through Goat River to Powell Lake, and home. But finally, I can cross No Name off my list of places I want to visit and ride, however so short.

No Name View

Chapter 15

Unexpected Destinations
Beartooth

Sometimes, the greatest adventures are the unexpected ones when you end up somewhere unforeseen. During recent decades, Margy and I have learned the joy of starting out on a trip without a solid destination, and seeing what happens.

Often, our biggest successes in this regard occur when flying our Piper Arrow from its home base in Bellingham, Washington. It's not unusual for us to takeoff without a specific destination in mind, finally making our decision 50 miles (or more) from the airport. We might begin a flight southbound – typical for departures from Bellingham, since it takes us towards Puget Sound and is pleasantly oriented along the ocean shoreline. After settling down in cruise, we'll often discuss where we'd like to go based on the visible cloud conditions and winds aloft, best observed from our perch a mile above the earth.

Since most of our flying is under instrument flight rules (IFR), it's necessary to initially file a destination, but for us it's often only a placeholder in our IFR flight plan. Thus, one of our first communications with air traffic control (ATC) involves our newly resolved destination: "Seattle Approach Control, Arrow Niner-Niner-Seven has a request for a change of destination."

ATC usually replies without question: "Approved, as requested." And off we go for a night of camping under our wing at an airport that meets our current "flight of fancy."

(These days, due to terrorism threats, there are certain destination changes that are questioned by ATC, but a quick explanation is all that's needed: "We've decided to stop overnight at Siletz Bay." With an immediate reply of "Approved, as requested.")

Some of the greatest destinations in our flying adventures have been places we didn't even intend to visit. Or in other cases, weather factors force a change of itinerary that results in experiencing locations we never would have chosen otherwise. (*Up the Airway*, Chapters 4 and 8; *Flying the Pacific Northwest*, Chapter 7).

A similar occurrence while traveling in our barge leads us to one of our greatest riding experiences on Powell Lake. After a rainy weekend that originally included plans to take our quads to the Head of Powell Lake with John, we try to salvage our preparations. The barge is ready to go, and so are we, if only the weather would cooperate. Sunday morning dawns questionable, although the forecast is for clearing and diminishing winds. By mid-morning, conditions improve, and we launch for a trip north with no specific destination in mind except a loose plan.

"Suppose we start north, and just see what happens," I suggest to Margy.

"Sure, let's do it," she replies.

After all these years, I shouldn't be surprised by Margy's flexibility when it comes to traveling. She enjoys unexpected destinations as much as I do. But winds are still swirling in Hole in the Wall, which could indicate rough conditions elsewhere on the lake. But the waves are smaller than expected, and soon we're settled down in slow cruise along Goat Island's shore.

"What do you think about taking a look at Beartooth?" I ask. "Could be windy up there, but we can always deviate to Olsen's Landing or turn around and off-load at Clover Dock."

"Sure," she replies without hesitation.

This will be a day trip, so we haven't packed any food except snacks. I'm at the helm today, navigating close to Goat Island so we can get a good look at the float cabins as we cruise north. In our slow barge, we feel comfortable tucked in close to shore, since our minimal wake won't damage cabin booms.

Although our destination today is still not confirmed, I've been thinking about Beartooth a lot lately. Ever since last month, when we stopped there during a boat trip with John, I've wanted to try riding this previously-closed main. Western Forest Products plans to reactive this logging road soon, and they've already positioned a surveyor's pickup truck at the site. When John, Margy, and I stepped off the Beartooth dock last month, we couldn't see very far up the main, and the barge ramp looked rough and in need of attention.

Since John had arrived at the dock with no shoes (and none aboard our boat, not unusual for John during the summer), we didn't explore the lower end of the road, although he trudged with us (*Ouch, ouch, ouch!*) a little ways past the truck, and then over to the bedraggled barge ramp (more *Ouch, ouch, ouch*).

"Probably all overgrown," notes John, referring to the lower part of the main we can see from the surveyor's F250 pickup. "Hard to tell from here."

How does a guy end up all the way up the lake at Beartooth with no shoes, you ask? I have no adequate answer, except to say that John is John when it comes to summer. His feet are the toughest I've seen, but walking a deactivated logging road is a mighty high limit: *Ouch, ouch, ouch!*

Thus, we departed Beartooth that day, knowing little except that a surveyor's truck was sitting near the dock, undoubtedly brought in via barge. It's a very good sign to me, since this truck must be going somewhere (or going somewhere very soon).

(A few months later, Western Forest Products announces a change in their plans for this location. They abandon their original intensions regarding reactivating Beartooth Main, necessitated by the results if a financial analysis of the cost for road-building in this rugged terrain compared to the value of the lumber. The cost of getting to the logs puts a halt to their plans, at least for now.)

I remember my one and only trip up Beartooth Main with John. We traveled on off-road 100 cc motorcycles, and found the most gorgeous scenery of all time, as far as I'm concerned. That was over a decade ago, just before the logging company moved out of Beartooth.

So if we get a chance to take a closer look at Beartooth Main today, I'll be thrilled. I don't expect to be able to ride very far, and the barge ramp may be unusable, but it will be fun to give it a try. If we make it that far.

When we pass Harry's cabin, we see him out on his deck, waving to us. We wave back, and consider stopping to say hello, but we don't.

"Should have stopped," says Margy after we're past the boom entrance. "Harry looked like he was waiting for us to turn in."

"Probably," I say. "But we can stop on our way home, if it's not too close to sunset."

Right now, I'm anxious to see what we're going to find at Beartooth. Even without a definite destination, I know I'm becoming obsessed with the possibilities of riding Beartooth Main, even if it's only possible for a few hundred metres.

After passing Harry's place, the next peninsula is bulging with several ready-to-tow booms of logs near Clover Dock, in position for the trip down Powell Lake to Block Bay. I navigate around the point to take a look at the dock.

"Nobody here today," says Margy.

"So we can come back if we can't off-load at Beartooth or the water at Olsen's Landing is too rough."

So in a way, I'm outlining some details to our evolving plan.

"What's our shortest quad ride so far this year?" I ask Margy as we turn north again, pulling away from the Clover Dock.

I know she remembers the ride I'm thinking about, only a few weeks ago.

"No Name," she replies immediately.

I nod in agreement, a smile coming to both of our faces. We rode only a few hundred metres, but it was fun adding No Name (on Goat Lake) to our list of places visited (Chapter 14).

"Could be even shorter at Beartooth," I suggest.

"Not a problem for me."

It's quite simple to off-load and then almost immediately on-load our quads from the barge. We've become experts in recent months. And short rides (although preferably longer than a few klicks) are okay with us.

It is then that I remember what I've left behind – my chainsaw. Here we are, approaching a logging road of unknown condition, and our trip may be stopped almost immediately by a fallen tree. It only takes one tree to stop our quads, unless we can cut our way through.

When we departed Hole in the Wall, I hadn't fully formulated plans for Beartooth, since this was a trip with an unknown destination, but I should have considered taking a chain saw. It's a simple accessory to add to my quad box, and I've made this blunder too many times. True, I thought we'd be riding on a trail today at Olsen's or Goat Island, and it wouldn't be a disappointment to have to turn around because of a small fallen tree. But going all the way to Beartooth, only to turn around because I left my chainsaw behind – what a shame. Next time… but I never seem to learn.

The winds have remained calm, and the broad channel abeam Olsen's Landing isn't even a bit choppy, conditions seldom found here. The exposed barge ramp at Beartooth would be problematic in strong winds, so everything seems set up for success. Even better news – from just offshore Beartooth, the barge ramp looks less rough than when we saw it last month, although I doubt anything has changed.

"Looks pretty good, don't you think?" I ask Margy.

"Deeper, too," she replies. "Maybe because of the lower lake level."

That probably sounds backwards, but the ramp's drop-off is often deeper close to shore during lower lake levels.

The ramp area looks so good that I don't even hesitate as we approach. I simply keep driving towards the rocky shore. Margy goes out on the bow, checking for underwater obstacles, but she never signals me once to deviate from my course. In fact, the depth sounder alarm doesn't even activate before contacting the gravel, since the stern is still in water that's plenty deep.

The barge ramp hasn't been improved since our last visit, but it's fully adequate for us. The dilapidated dock still floats nearby in disrepair, but it and the ramp will be some of the first improvements once surveying and road-building goes into high gear. The fact that both the dock are ramp are still unimproved means we shouldn't expect much from the road today. This could be a trip shorter than No Name.

Off-load of our quads in the sizeable rocks is easy. I'm always amazed how easily these rugged machines navigate rough terrain. We ride up past the surveyor's white pickup truck, and stop to look back at the ramp where we've tied up the barge. This is an acceptable place to leave the boat, since it's unlikely anyone else will visit this secluded spot today.

Barge Ramp at Beartooth

Margy leads as we climb the initial hill from the truck, but I almost immediately turn off my headlights, our mutual signal that I want her to stop. She sees my cue in her rearview mirror almost immediately, and comes to a halt. I pull up behind her, get off my quad, and step to the rear of my bike. I can see Margy is watching me closely, wondering what I'm doing.

I open the rear box and pull out my can of bear spray, holding it high for her to see: "It's Beartooth, you know!" I yell over the sound of our idling engines.

I can't see inside her helmet and tinted goggles, but Margy is undoubtedly laughing. She nods in acknowledgement, and we start back up the hill.

The climb is unexpectedly easy, with small trees and bushes in the middle of the main, but almost nothing completely blocking our path. Our bikes push the small trees down, and we simply drive over them. However, within the first few hundred metres, we come to a big fallen branch. Margy stops, gets off her quad, and hauls the limb off to the side. I stand ready with my clippers, but they're not needed. Still, it reminds me we're unlikely to get away with this very far without a chainsaw. I could kick myself!

Surprisingly, this is the only obstacle we need to clear during today's ride. This old main has obviously been maintained on-and-off in the past decade, maybe because the logging company knows they're coming back sometime soon. It's probably easier to roughly maintain an old road than allow it to become completely inactive. In a remote location like this, there's little concern quads or motorcycles will try to use the old road (which is a liability concern for logging companies), so why not just keep it semi-active. Then again, the white pickup truck has done some of the recent repairs, as evidenced by occasional stacked rocks along the edge of the road where small washouts have occurred. It's probably a warning to themselves that there's a bad spot to avoid. And if a truck can maneuver along this road, it's even easier for a quad. Still, there are no recent tire tracks, so I'm not sure how far the surveyors have gone.

Margy leads our climb without hesitation. The dropoff to Beartooth Creek on our right is substantial, but covered with small

Margy on Beartooth Main

trees and bushes. In her mind, what she can't see can't hurt her. So we progress rapidly up the main.

Small glaciers in hanging valleys make for a scenic ride, although it's obvious these ice fields have shrunk within their glacier-cut cirques. Like seasonally shrinking Powell Lake, these glaciers leave a noticeable bathtub ring marking their recent larger girth. I'm not sure they will make it through the summer, and then they may be gone forever (at least as far as "forever" is envisioned by earth's current inhabitants).

The scenery is spectacular. In fact, it's at least as sublime as I remember from years ago on my motorbike. Mountains rise abruptly, clouds surround most of the peaks, and rough granite slopes and glaciers add to the spectacle. I was afraid my second trip on Beartooth Main wouldn't match my initial feeling of wonder, but I was wrong. This is even better than the first time.

At the first major bridge, we stop for a photo of Margy in front of the waterfalls. This dry summer has undoubtedly affected the level of flow, but it's still impressive.

Margy at Waterfalls on Beartooth Main

We continue up the main, turning west at the hairpin course reversal where the road heads back towards Powell Lake. We cross another bridge and a smaller waterfall, where the bushes in the road become thicker. It's still passible, but I know the main will soon reach a dead-end. It's not worth pushing any farther, since we've seen the best part of this gorgeous valley.

We stop for a snack of nuts and still-cool water from our ice pack. Then we turn around, and start back down Beartooth Main. I may never find a more beautiful location to ride. For this one trip alone, it's been worth equipping a barge for quad adventures. Yet we've seen so much more while barging around on Powell Lake. I psychologically pat myself on the back. Barge, quads -- what a good mix.

Chapter 16

The Head
Head of Powell Lake

For many local riders, the Head of Powell Lake is considered the ultimate quad destination on the lake. However, few are able to ride there, since quads don't fit into most recreational boats. It's the farthest north you can go on the lake; by definition, the most remote location. And the extensive logging roads emanating from the Head provide a network of mains unrivaled elsewhere on the lake. I've ridden there twice with John, once on 100 cc motorcycles (transported in our boat), and later by quad (via a log raft pushed by my Campion). It has been five years since my raft-quad trip, and it will be difficult to equal that adventure (*Beyond the Main*, Chapter 1 – 3). But I want to try, and this time I'm determined to include Margy in the experience.

John, Margy, and I have been waiting for the right time, but it seems to elude us. To match our schedules with the weather (a weekend trip is necessary due to logging activity), we plan several targeted dates, only to cancel for one reason or another. The reason is usually related to weather.

However, John has come up with a new plan involving a weekday trip for him and his friend, Mike. They're both avid hikers, and want to try to summit the ridge behind Cypress Main, one of the roads at the Head that isn't currently involved with log hauling. When Mike gets a three-day break from his job at the paper mill, they quickly put their plan together, borrowing the barge to transport their quads. It's a major undertaking involving two diverse individuals trying to consolidate their camping equipment and food provisions.

John and Mike Load the Barge at Cabin Number 3

"It looks like you're going for three weeks, rather than three days," I tease, as they finish loading the barge at my cabin.

Mike shrugs in a way that implies it's all John's fault. In reality, they both want to take every amenity to make their trip comfortable.

The previous day, I drove the barge to the Shinglemill to load their quads, and now they've arrived at my cabin by early-morning boat to transfer their supplies to the barge and launch on their trip.

By 9 am, they're on their way, and I'm thrilled they've finally matched this trip to their schedules. Margy and I plan to go to the Head the following weekend, probably with John, even though he'll have just returned from this hiking adventure. We'll need a weekend with its limited logging activity to ride freely on the four major mains at the Head.

* * * * *

JOHN'S HIKING TRIP GOES WELL. Although he and Mike are not able to climb all the way to the ridge above the top of Cypress Main, they make it most of the way, and they're able to do plenty of riding on the other mains, regardless of the weekday logging activity. However, sleeping in a tent is always a challenge for John, and he's exhausted after fitful slumber during the trip. I'm not surprised when he announces he'll stay home this weekend and try to recover. So Margy and I will be on our own, but we're already prepared to go. So, reluctantly, leaving John behind, we decide to continue as planned.

On Friday morning, we depart our cabin at 9 o'clock, knowing our itinerary will get us to the Head before the week's logging is concluded. But we can progress northward leisurely and simply wait at the dock until the loggers secure their equipment and depart in their crew boats.

As always, we consider a trip like this as a camping (and relaxing) trip, as much as a quad trip, so arriving at the Head early isn't a problem. And it should allow us to avoid the strong up-lake winds typically encountered later in the day. The barge handles well in rough conditions, but that doesn't mean it's pleasant travel when the waves are lapping over the bow. We expect our travel time from Hole in the Wall to the Head to be approximately three hours, with numerous logging docks available along the way, in case windy conditions develop.

The trip north is spectacular, weaving through the steep fjord-like landscape beyond Beartooth. Conditions remain as good as can be expected, with a rough patch from Goat Island's Clover Dock to abeam Olsen's Landing. Then it's only small waves the rest of the way, with the typical daytime up-lake southerly breeze after passing Beartooth.

With our zig-zag sightseeing route, it still takes only a little over three hours. After Beartooth, we pass close to Billy Goat Main, looking over the dock and barge ramp for possible future exploration. John says the road has been "severely deactivated," which means deep quad-eating trenches. Additionally, a bridge has been pulled out, making the main unrideable. But things change fast as logging activity adjusts to new harvesting areas, and this steep road will likely be open again in the near future.

Another deviation takes us to the Jim Brown barge ramp, where John and Mike camped earlier in the week. The dock at the Head was crowded with crew boats when they arrived, so they came ashore here, setting up their tents next to the barge.

We pull into the Head's dock shortly after noon, to find two crew boats and a smaller forestry management boat. This smaller vessel stimulates my memory, since this is *Daniels Lady*, the same one used

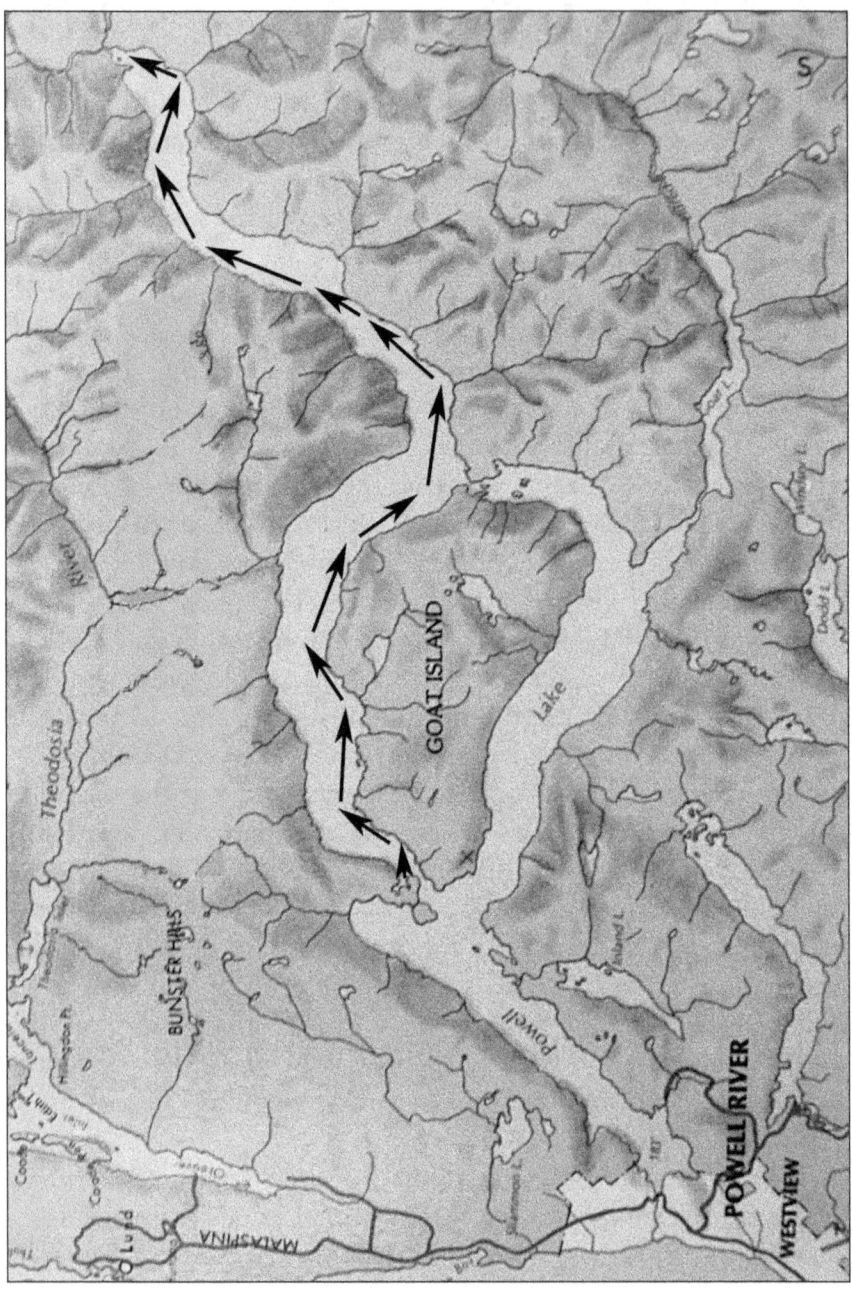

To the Head

by surveyors I met during my trip here with John on the raft five years ago. We encountered this boat and its occupants several times that trip, and I wonder if it might be the same crew.

There's plenty of room for one more boat, so we tie up to the dock. Here we'll await the end of the logging shift, and then off-load our quads. Typically, loggers begin their day early, passing Hole in the Wall at about 5 am on hot, summer days, and finishing in mid-afternoon. Meanwhile, Margy and I are content to bask in our folding chairs, reading our books and sipping on ice-cold Cokes.

When the crew of the *Chuck Forest* returns to their boat at about 2 o'clock, I'm absorbing the sun and cat-napping in my chair. These are shake blockers who cut otherwise-discarded cedar logs to eventually produce wood shingles. This is the beginning of their weekend, so they quickly prepare to depart. When I ask about their schedule, they say they won't return until Monday.

A few minutes later, a red Bell Jet Ranger helicopter swoops in from the high ridge to the east. The chopper carries two loggers who've been working in the Eldred Valley. It's faster to take the crew boat home to Powell River from the Head of Powell Lake than to travel by truck from the Eldred's land-based staging area near Goat Lake.

As the Jet Ranger takes off again, the two loggers come down the bridge to the dock, hauling their chain saws and logging gear. In just a few minutes these young fellows are diving into the lake, cooling off

Barge with *Daniels Lady* (right) and Chuck Forest (left)

Bell Helicopter at the Head

after a hot workday in the forest. Ten minutes later, two men arrive in a pickup truck, walking down to the forestry management boat, *Daniels Lady*. These fellows are as young as the two loggers, but look more academic than athletic.

"I bet you're surveyors," I say in introduction.

"Timber cruisers," says the youngest fellow. "About the same thing."

"I don't suppose you remember meeting two quad riders here five years ago? We were pushing a log raft with a boat, and we met the crew of *Daniels Lady* here at the Head."

"Not me," says the younger fellow. "I've only been working here for a year."

"Nor me," says the other man. "But I've been timber cruising longer than that."

"I guess *Daniels Lady* has been around a long time."

"As long as I can remember," replies the older fellow.

"Are all of the roads in good enough condition for us to ride this weekend?" I ask.

"No problem. They're in pretty good shape. We've been on most of them."

"You know, it's funny," I say. "I bet you were happy as you descended from your last survey route today, headed back to your boat, getting ready for some time off. Meanwhile, in my free time, I come all the way up the lake to explore the same places where you work."

"Oh, it's new and amazing to me, too," replies the younger man. "I just love it."

I can see the gleam in the older man's eyes, too. It's a tremendous environment for "work." Yet, it's hard physical labour, especially for the fallers. But imagine traveling home from work in a combination of Jet Ranger and crew boat. Or being the pilot who flies the helicopter into this challenging terrain under almost any weather condition.

Daniels Lady departs, and the Jet Ranger is back again, dropping two more loggers, and immediately heads north to pick up two additional men working up Daniels Main. When the chopper returns again, there's a short pause while the helicopter pilot and the newly arrived crew members secure the helicopter for the night.

Quickly, the entire team (six loggers and the pilot) is aboard *Shamahawk*, a skookum metal crew boat with hefty twin outboards. Almost immediately, the engines are running, ready to go. But there's a brief delay while the chopper pilot hops off the boat and runs back up the ramp to retrieve something from the helicopter, accompanied by multiple catcalls from *Shamahawk's* deck. These loggers don't take too kindly to anyone delaying their end-of-day trip home, so the pilot breaks into a trot. They give him similar treatment as he returns down the ramp, carrying his expensive flight helmet: "Come on! Come on!"

The moment the pilot steps aboard, *Shamahawk* pulls away from the dock. Some of this crew will return here to work here throughout the weekend. But for now, it's suddenly very quite. We're alone, and the Head is ours.

By now, the up-lake breeze has brewed into a sizable wind, so we decide to delay our barge reconfiguration a little longer. There's no need to ride today, so we can off-load our quads and set up our tent later. Our remote privacy is plenty of entertainment. For several hours, we sit in our lawn chairs, reading and soaking up some sun.

We eat an early dinner of chicken-n-noodles and salad, and by then the wind has abated to almost nothing. So we unhook from the dock, and off-load our quads at the easily-accessed ramp. Then we motor the barge the short distance back to the dock, and set up our tent on the deck, in its anti-bear configuration. No sensible bear would go to the trouble of clambering down the ramp to the dock and then climb aboard the flat bed of our barge to investigate. Of course, just in case, we've secured all of our food in the cab.

* * * * *

IN THE MORNING, I AWAKE AT 6 AM to the sound of *Shamahawk* returning to the dock for a weekend of continued heli-logging on upper Daniels Main. A few minutes later, two pickup trucks depart, and the Jet Ranger roars to life, warming up its powerful turbine engine, and then takes off.

We fall back asleep, awakened again when sunlight begins to pour into the tent. We'd like to get going early enough to take advantage of the cool temperatures on the roads, so we're out of the tent fairly promptly. Breakfast is a typical camping menu of cereal, toast, hard-boiled eggs, and coffee. We're on the road by 9 o'clock.

Near the first milepost (designated in miles rather than kilometres here) a sign advises: "Rock Slide – Do not stop next 50 metres." We slow down through this somewhat obstacle-filled portion of the road, but pass through easily. Nevertheless, it makes me wonder if this is an indicator of what we can expect today.

In fact, in the next two days, we'll find most of the roads in good shape, although washouts or encroaching bushes and trees eventually block many of them towards their upper reaches. Generally, this is one of the easiest areas to ride in the entire region, undoubtedly because the lower sections of all the roads are maintained for recurring logging activity.

Farther up Daniels Main, we encounter a parked flatbed truck with door markings of *Goat Lake Forest Products*. It sits at the turnout where the shake blockers we met yesterday have been working. So we turn off, and climb a short distance to a slash where big cedar blocks (shakes) have been cut and stacked neatly on pallets. It looks like a giant's pile of winter firewood. These blocks will be even more

Shake Blocks

valuable when cut into cedar shingles for construction of roofs and siding.

Back on the main, we climb alongside overhead power lines constructed a decade ago by controversial Plutonic Power, diverting run-of-river electrical power from Toba Inlet to Vancouver and eventually to the States. At the time, recreational ATV riders, hikers, and conservationists expressed doubts about the impact on the environment and the recreational trails in the region. The lines crossing the Head of Powell Lake (and then up-and-over the ridge to the Eldred River and Goat Main) are reminders of the old dispute between the power company and locals. Some opponents suggested grizzlies and mountain lions would follow the path south towards Powell River (which they have, but not only because of the new route). As time eventually soothed people's concerns, original objections subsided.

Today's ride is a sad reminder that this is one of the driest summers on record. Waterfalls, so prevalent in this area, have been reduced to a mere trickle. Only dry rocks remain under Daniels Main's numerous bridges where roaring tributaries used to feed into nearby Daniels River. That explains the shallow, lethargic flow of the river itself. The landscape is still majestic, but lacks the brilliant reflections from sparkling water that normally tumbles over mountainous granite escarpments.

At an odometer reading of 16 kilometres (mileposts are now mostly hidden by roadside bushes), a tire-tracked turnoff to the left marks the access road for the heli-logging crew. We drive a short distance up the spur, but are stopped almost immediately by a rope strung across the road, with a sign indicating active logging. We turn around, continue back to the intersection, and start up the old main again. Road conditions quickly deteriorate, and we encounter the first landslide.

We easily navigate this obstruction, but the next washout is a bigger challenge. Margy asks me to take her bike through a rutted corner that makes her uncomfortable. I remember helping John and his friends rebuild this portion of the trail a decade ago. We laid a corduroy-style path of logs that's still in pretty good shape today.

Less than a klick beyond the second difficult spot, with my tripmeter reading 20 kilometres, the road becomes almost unusable. A major stream roared across the main, probably last winter as judged by the freshness of the washout. The road is indiscernible, but a trace of the old main is visible on the far uphill side of this gigantic swath of rocks and boulders. I start through tentatively, stopping here and there to move mid-sized rocks to make the footing safe for my quad. Meanwhile, I've left Margy behind in a shady spot, with a walkie-talkie, our can of bear spray, and a promise not to be gone too long. In fact, I doubt I'll be able to push forward very far. Usually, if you find a major obstacle on a main, you might as well turn around right away. Otherwise, you can expect to find more and more barriers ahead.

In this case, I work my way through the rock-strewn path, with a usable old trail on the other side. Around the next corner, I encounter a tree across the road, but I'm barely able to sneak under it on the high side. However, within less than a kilometre, I'm stopped by a cross-ditch that's too big to traverse. I think I can rebuild this part of the trail by filling it in with rocks, and I start to do so. Then I reconsider the situation – this wouldn't be a good place to get stuck, solo with a long walk back to Margy. Plus, I'm nearly certain there are more obstacles ahead. No one has been through here in years.

"I'm turning around now," I tell Margy on the walkie-talkie.

"Good," she says, and I think I hear relief in her voice.

* * * * *

WE RIDE BACK DOWN DANIELS MAIN, and take a left turn onto Powell Main, where we stop on the bridge crossing the Daniels River. A little farther up the road, we parallel Powell River in an uphill climb between beautiful granite peaks.

Eventually, we come to an intersection where a newly constructed road peals off to the right. It's a steep entry, so Margy elects to wait while I explore the new main. She's content to wait behind with her walkie-talkie, always carrying a good book and her camera for times like this.

The new road winds upward, first in ready-to-use condition, and then it progresses through various stages of construction. I approach the just-pushing-through phase after riding 2 kilometres. The main runs next to a steep cliff, where it's been necessary to blast through

Daniels River on Powell Main

extensive sections of granite. The smooth sandy road changes to darker, hard-packed dirt, and finally I come to the first scattering of construction vehicles, several trucks and a tall bucketed crane. Beyond here, the road's foundation is rough rock, until I come to a corner with another set of vehicles with tank-like treads for initial work on the unfinished stretch of the road.

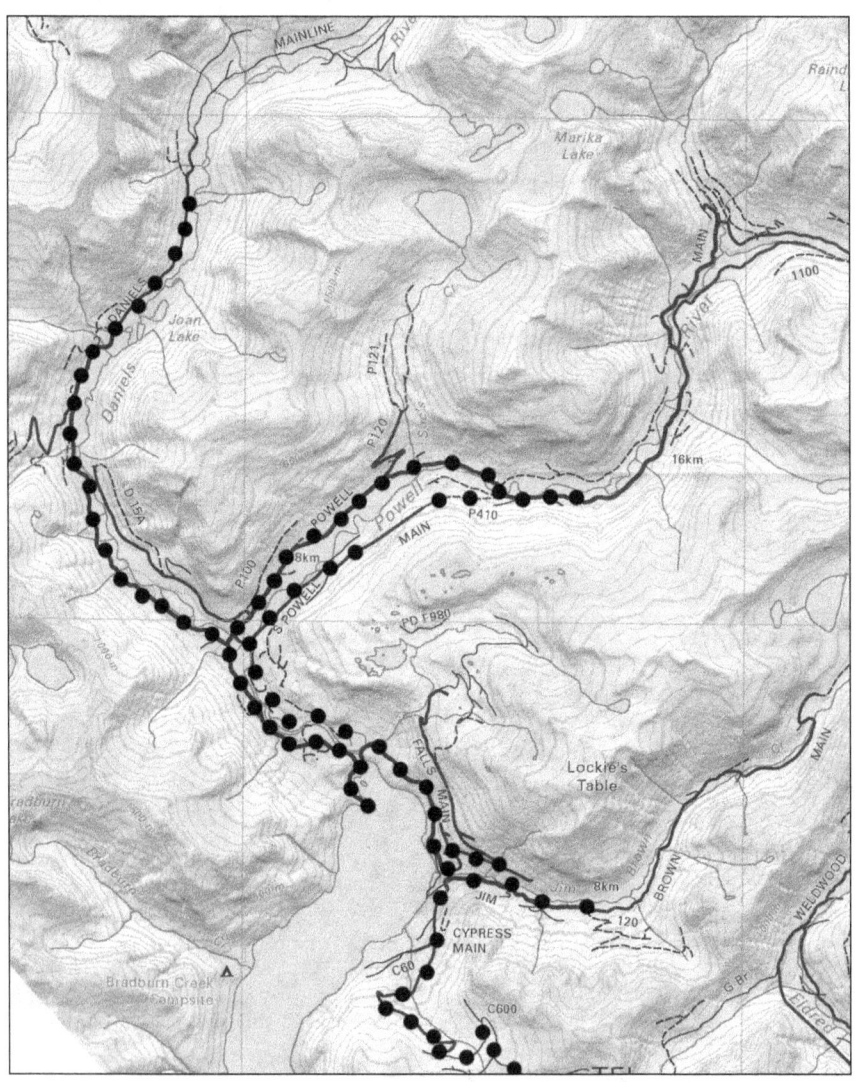

Main Roads at the The Head

Although I can see the intended path of the main beyond the curve, I can't ride any farther. Quickly, the surface deteriorates to a jumbled mix of boulders and logs positioned to form the foundation of the new road. Soon it will be covered with smaller rocks and then dirt, packed to form a smooth, hard surface. It's an interesting visual lesson in logging road construction, sequential time slices of a major construction project.

After I return to the junction where Margy waits, we travel only a short distance farther up Powell Main to the place where it deteriorates into an old overgrown road that's no more than a trail too narrow for a quad. According to the map, we've come less than halfway to the end of the road, but nature has reclaimed everything from here to the end. Thus, it's time to turn around and head back to the barge.

We pull into the staging area near the dock at about 4 o'clock. The helicopter is parked, and *Shamahawk* is gone. I pick a spot about 20 metres past Margy in the parking area, pull in close to the dock ramp, and turn off my engine. As I remove my helmet, Margy yells to me.

"Are you throwing rocks?"

"What do you mean?" I yell back.

"I thought I heard a rock hit between us."

Clunk! A small piece of wood hits the ground only a few metres from my quad.

"No, and I'm not throwing wood either!" I exclaim.

There's only one explanation.

"John!" I yell.

Sure enough, John comes around from behind one of the trucks, laughing: "Gotcha!" he yells.

At first, I can't believe John is here. Then I realize this is just like him. A few days ago, he said he might take his boat to the Head this weekend to try to find us. Margy suggested he should stop at Hole in the Wall, if he decided to make the trip. At the Hole he could transfer to our Hewescraft for a more comfortable ride north.

Surprise! – John is everywhere.

"Do you want to go explore a beach I found?" asks John after we've relaxed at the dock with some cold drinks. "The water's so low that

Barge and Hewescraft at the Head

Jim Brown Beach with Author at the Bow of the Hewescraft

there's a new sandy beach where Jim Brown Creek pours out into the lake. Should be good swimming there."

So off we go to explore a beach that hasn't existed in several years, driving the metal Hewescraft carefully onto the shallow sandy shore a kilometre south of the dock at the Head. We (Bro, too!) explore the exposed lakebed, and swim in surprisingly warm water, a fitting finale to an inspiring and dusty day of quad riding at the Head.

* * * * *

THAT EVENING, LIKE CLOCKWORK DURING THE SUMMER, the up-lake winds suddenly stop at sunset, reversing an hour later to a northerly flow down from the high mountains. It's a textbook example of valley winds during the day (up the lake) and mountain winds at night (cooler air pouring downhill). In British Columbia's fjord-like inlets they're called inflow (or upslope) winds during the day and outflows at night. Powell Lake, although a cut-off freshwater inlet, is exactly the same.

In the middle of the night, the northerly wind peaks, splashing water under the barge's hull ribs in a noisy, metallic sloshing sound. We eventually get used to it, and get back to sleep. It's the same both nights at the Head, but fitful sleep is better than abandoning our tent's anti-bear position on the barge.

The next morning, we ride the four remaining mains at the Head. In the span of a weekend, we're able to travel most of the easily navigable ATV routes in this remarkable location. It's a lot of territory to cover. But I'm already imagining returning in the spring to see this terrain when the flow of water returns, dropping endless waterfalls from the mountain slopes, and filling the dry creeks to roaring capacity. It will be a completely different setting.

We ride up South Powell Main, which parallels Powell River on the other side. The Head has experienced nearly continual logging since the early 1900s, so the roads remain in amazingly good condition compared to logging mains closer to town. Here on South Powell Main, we find the road wide and comfortable. Conditions are smooth enough for me to ride most of the weekend in the "slot" position, a few metres behind and to the left of Margy. I drop back behind her when approaching curves, just in case, even though there's no one else on these roads this weekend, as evidenced by only the *Shamarock* at the dock, and its heli-logging crew up Daniels Main. Slot riding keeps me out of the dusty swirl from Margy's quad. It's a lot safer to ride like this here than on other mains with their occasional traffic. For our two days of riding at the Head, we never see another moving vehicle or person on the Head's six main roads.

Today, starting up South Powell Main, we pass a big yellow bus that serves as a hunter's cabin, but not this weekend. Then we ride beside the river, where John and I stopped to visit his secret spot on Powell River years ago. Somewhere along here we parked our quads, but it's well beyond my ability to recognize where we bushwhacked our way to the river (*Beyond the Main*, Chapter 2). Finally, after kilometres of wide logging road, Margy and I encounter a rope across the main and a sign: *Active Falling*.

"Obviously, no falling today," I say to Margy when I pull to a stop. "But we'll turn around."

"Sure," replies Margy. "They probably don't want anyone messing with their harvesting machines."

It's true – loggers are less concerned with recreational riders using their roads than tinkering with their equipment. I don't blame them.

When we exit South Powell Main, we turn left to parallel the lake's eastern shoreline. I almost immediately come to a screeching halt. Margy sees me in her rearview mirror and comes back to investigate.

"Fresh tracks," I say, showing her what I've found on the side of the road. "Big bear."

"Really fresh," she replies. "But how did the bear get on and off the road."

She's right. The tracks suddenly appear, run for a few metres, and then disappear. There's a ditch to the side, and a low cliff above it, but no bear is going to bound up and down a cliff just for a quick sprint on the road. We discuss it some more, but never decide how this could be. It must remain a mystery of the forest.

At the junction with Falls Main, we turn left and follow it uphill. We pass the spot where I wiped out on my 100 cc motorcycle while traveling with John years ago (*Up the Main*, Chapter 18). It's fun to recognize old landmarks in the wilderness – so familiar, yet so different as time goes by. Higher up, there's a new logging slash where John and I hiked down to the old yellow cedar snow survey cabin. It wasn't easy

Bear Tracks

to get to the cabin then. Now it looks impossible. Passing benchmarks like this reminds me how few people (other than loggers) get to travel the extensive roads at the Head. What a privilege it is to be here.

Above the slash, Falls Main quickly deteriorates. With no active logging, the road quickly disappears, and it's not worth the effort to continue. So we turn around and descend to find nearby Jim Brown Main. Soon we're headed uphill again in good road conditions that gradually deteriorate. We pass a huge old growth fir topped with healthy-looking branches and a moss-permeated canopy. This is one of the few places in our region where you can visit old growth trees easily by quad. Most of the region surrounding Powell Lake was logged in the early 1900s, and second-growth or younger trees are all that remain, except in a few spots where loggers intentionally left behind a few old growth giants.

One last logging road remains today. I somewhat nervously scan the bushes as we exit Jim Brown and start up the lower reaches of Cypress Main. Entrenched in my mind is another memory from my previous quad trip here with John – a grizzly standing his ground in the middle of the road (on two legs, as grizzlies tend to stand when defending their territory). There are no bears in sight today (but there were those big tracks, so fresh).

The grizzly encounter with John remains as one of my most memorable wildlife incidents. It's right up there with my recollection of a bear swimming across Powell Lake and a mountain lion stalking John, Bro, and me near Heather Main (*Off the Grid*, Chapter 17). If you hike or bike in this region for very long, you're sure to collect memories of wildlife that are more enchanting than threatening.

Today, we make it as far as the big bridge on Cypress Main, where waterfall with granite chutes and pools below the bridge captures our attention. Looking ahead to the other side of the bridge, Margy is quick to stand her ground.

"That's it," she says. "I can see there's a climb I'm not going to like."

"No problem," I reply.

We knew this was coming because the end of Cypress Main is one of the steepest roads at the Head, and it goes the highest.

"You go on," she says. "I'll wait here. Pretty place."

So again, we discuss our simple plan, with my promise to keep her posted via walkie-talkie, and to be careful.

It's farther to the top than I remembered. Cypress Main goes on and on, and up and up. But the road is in generally good condition, so much so that I must remind myself repeatedly to slow down. The worst danger here is to hit an obstacle in the road and lose control, or damage the bike. Yes, we have walkie-talkies for communication, but Margy wouldn't be able to easily drive up here to assist me. We're a long way from home, and *Shamahawk* has probably already departed the dock. There's no one else within about 20 kilometres, and no way to communicate anyway.

So I'm careful for all 9 kilometres of my travel up Cypress Main from the bridge. The road climbs and winds and climbs some more. Near the top, I find the spur to the right where John and Mike rode to the end a few days ago, and then began their climb toward a ridge o overlook the Eldred Valley. Quad tracks confirm they were here, maybe the only other quads this summer.

From this spur, they hiked up towards the ridge, hoping to break into the open above the tree line, where the going would be easier. It

Lower Viewpoint on Cypress Main

was at about that height, after a grueling climb, that they ran out of energy and time nearly simultaneously, and turned around and hiked back down to their quads, missing their goal by only a few hundred metres.

I ride the spur for a while, until the cross-trenches get bigger, and I begin to worry about breaking an axle. And I'm probably now out of line-of-sight communication with Margy. So I return to the main, and continue upward to the end, where the road terminates in a jumble of logs piled after logging ended.

I take a break, getting off my quad, drinking water, and enjoying the view, but leaving the motor running as a safety precaution. From up here, I might be able to contact Margy.

"Hello, from way up here," I transmit over the walkie-talkie.

"Hello, from back down here," Margy replies.

"I'm at the top. Took longer than I expected, but the road is good."

"Good view?" she asks.

"Not bad," I reply. "Kind of stark and remote. But pretty."

"Pretty down here, too," she responds.

"Coming down now."

"See you soon."

I click off the radio to save the batteries, just in case. Then I get back on my quad, ready to start down Cypress Main.

After one of our most memorable riding weekends of all time, we're headed back to the barge. The ride we've looked forward to for years is ending, for now. But we'll be back, to explore some of the same places in different conditions. Riding is like that, for the mountains and the forests forever cast an ever-changing hue, and never cease to inspire.

About the Author

From 1980 to 2005, Wayne Lutz was Chairman of the Aeronautics Department at Mount San Antonio College in Los Angeles. The author also served 20 years as a U.S. Air Force C-130 aircraft maintenance officer. His educational background includes a B.S. degree in physics from the University of Buffalo and an M.S. in systems management from the University of Southern California. He is a flight instructor with 7000 hours of flying experience.

The author resides in a floating cabin on Canada's Powell Lake in all seasons, and occasionally in a city-folk condo in Bellingham, Washington. His writing genres include regional Canadian publications and science fiction. This is his fourth book regarding off-road riding in coastal British Columbia. Contact the author at wlutz@mtsac.edu

Author interviewing Bro on his quad in Theodosia Valley

Geographic Index

Beartooth Main/Beartooth Mountain   p.49, 177 - 178, 180 - 184
Chippewa Bay   p.86, 88 - 89, 115
Chippewa Main   p.69, 89
Chippewa North   p.69, 130 - 136, 147, 151 - 154
Chippewa South   p.50 - 56, 109, 114 - 116, 122, 147 - 149,
Clover Lake   p.101, 140
Clover Main/Clover Dock   p.41, 63, 69, 99 - 102, 113 - 114, 117 - 118, 130, 137, 139, 150
Cypress Main   p.186, 201 - 204
D-Branch   p.173 -174
Dagleish Main   p.145
Daniels Main   p.192 - 195
Daniels River   p.195
Dianne Main   p.25, 29
Dunn Main/Dun Dock   p.59, 62, 83 - 84, 112, 114 - 115, 116 - 118, 123 -124
Donkey Trail   p.87, 91 - 95
Eldred River   p.25, 29 - 30
Elvis Main   p.102 - 104
Elvis Point   p.98
Falls Main   p.200
Fiddlehead Farm   p.38, 71, 73 - 75
First Narrows   p.59, 85, 96, 150
Giovanno Lake   p.76
Giovanno Main   p.77
Goat Lake   p.168 - 170
Goat Main   p.23 - 26, 30, 33 -35, 171 -172
Goat River   p.15 - 16, 82, 167
Goat 1   p.31 - 33
Goat 2   p.31 - 33
Haslam Lake   p.38, 71, 76

Geographic Index

Heather Main   p.89 - 90
Jim Brown Main   p.187, 201
Kinsman's Beach   p.58, 110, 148
Last Chance Trail   p.87, 90
Lewis Lake   p.77
Mowat Bay   p.121 - 122
Museum Main   p.86, 111
Narrows   p.166
No Name Ramp   p.17, 108, 166, 168, 174 - 175
North Sea   p.59, 115
Olsen's Creek   p.104 - 105, 146
Olsen's Lake   p.106 - 107, 144
Olsen's Landing   p.105, 137 - 138, 141 - 142, 160 - 161
Olsen's Main   p.105, 143 - 145, 161 - 162
Pickle Point   p.72
Powell Lake Resort   p.141, 160
Powell Main   p.195 - 197
Rainbow Lodge   p.37 - 38, 42, 44
Rainbow Main   p.80 - 82
Second Narrows   p.41- 42
Shermans Main   p.37 - 38, 43 - 49
South Powell Main   p.199
Spire Lake   p.66 - 67, 124 - 126
Spire Main   p.63 - 70, 113 - 114, 118 - 119, 124 - 128
Squirrel Creek   p.23 - 24
Stump Creek   p.151
Theodosia Valley   p.153 - 157, 162 - 165
Tin Hat Mountain   p.77

Coastal British Columbia Stories

by Wayne J. Lutz

*Up the Lake
Up the Main
Up the Winter Trail
Up the Strait
Up the Airway
Farther Up the Lake
Farther Up the Main
Farther Up the Strait
Cabin Number 5
Off the Grid
Up the Inlet
Beyond the Main
Powell Lake by Barge and Quad*

Future Titles:
*Islands and Inlets
Beneath the Waters of Coastal BC*

Other Books by Wayne J. Lutz

Science Fiction Titles

Echo of a Distant Planet
Inbound to Earth
Across the Gallactic Sea
Anomaly at Fortune Lake
When Galaxies Collide

Pacific Northwest Series

Paddling the Pacific Northwest
Flying the Pacific Northwest

Powell Lake by Barge and Quad is the 13th in a series of volumes focusing on the unique places and memorable people of coastal British Columbia

Order at:
www.PowellRiverBooks.com

Coastal BC Living Blog
PowellRiverBooks.blogspot.com

www.ingramcontent.com/pod-product-compliance
Lightning Source LLC
Chambersburg PA
CBHW071731080526
44588CB00013B/1989